CLIMBING MY HIMALAYA

CLIMBING MY HIMALAYA

A JOURNEY THROUGH BROKENNESS TO GOD'S LOVE, HEALING, AND REDEMPTION

BY WENDY CHI

Share Your Story Ministry

COPYRIGHT

Share Your Story Ministry

Share Your Story Ministry

ISBN 979-8-9859266-0-6 (print book)
ISBN 979-8-9859266-1-3 (ebook)
ISBN 979-8-9859266-2-0 (audiobook)

Library of Congress Control Number: 2022904503
Publisher's Cataloging-in-Publication data

Names: Chi, Wendy, author.
Title: Climbing my Himalaya : a journey through brokenness to God's love , healing , and redemption / Wendy Chi.
Description: Saginaw, TX: Share Your Story Ministry, 2022.
Identifiers: LCCN: 2022904503 | ISBN: 979-8-9859266-0-6 (paperback) | 979-8-9859266-1-3 (ebook)
Subjects: LCSH Chi, Wendy. | Immigrant families--United States--Biography. | Taiwanese Americans--Biography. | Christian biography. | BISAC BIOGRAPHY & AUTOBIOGRAPHY / Personal Memoirs | RELIGION / Christian Living / Personal Memoirs
Classification: LCC BR1700.3 .C45 2022 | DDC 270.092/2--dc23

DEDICATION

To Dad and Mom for your dedication, commitment, and endless hard work to better the lives of others, including those of your children.

To Dora Chazarreta, who guided me to a support group that resulted in my reconciliation with God and who showed me by example how to give grace and unconditional love to others.

ACKNOWLEDGEMENTS

A special thanks to:

My mom, dad, brothers, and their wives for their encouragement and providing details of their experiences for this book.

My two daughters for being a joy in my life and for their patience during my book writing. I am also grateful for my ex-husband's love and care for my precious girls.

My divorce care facilitators for their love and care in letting me repeat the classes so many times during my time of healing.

My friends from the divorce care and reconciliation support group for your encouragement and love as I continue to heal.

Jill Duncan from *Helping Hands* class at *First Baptist Church of Saginaw* for working with me on my book draft and all her encouragement.

My editor Jeanette Windle, who could read my mind on many parts of this book in bringing my thoughts to the finalized manuscript.

My photo editor Michael Gonzales for restoring and editing my photos to help tell my story, for helping with my logos editing and for taking my author photos.

My publisher Amy Deardon and her team for patiently working and guiding me to the finished line.

Above all, I am deeply thankful to God for His relentless pursuit in loving and forgiving me through Jesus Christ and patience in the writing of this book as well as the comfort of God's Holy Spirit in my deepest valleys, healing my pain and giving me perspective of all the things for which I can be grateful regardless of circumstances.

TABLE OF CONTENTS

Taiwan, Republic of China

Important cities from my parents' story.

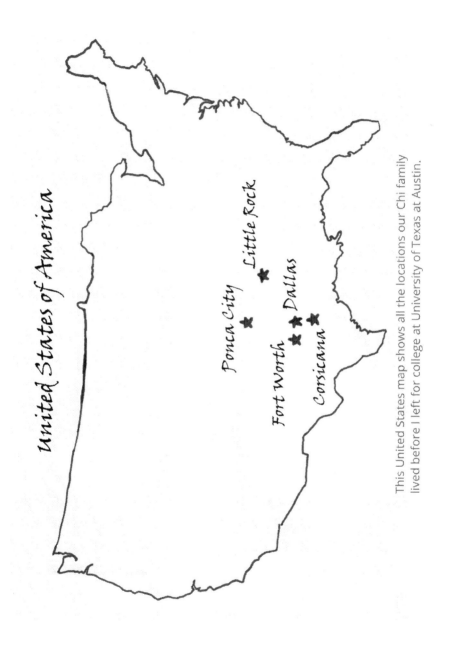

United States of America

Ponca City ★

Little Rock ★

Fort Worth ★ ★ Dallas

Corsicana ★

This United States map shows all the locations our Chi family lived before I left for college at University of Texas at Austin.

INTRODUCTION

信望愛

MY MOUNT HIMALAYA

Since 2013, God has been using many other people to confirm to me that I should write my story in book form. I have shared my family's journey many times over the years. When I've told my story to friends, they have often responded, "You should write a book to encourage others!"

I have hesitated to do so. English is not my native language, and writing is not my strength. I've allowed my doubts to limit me, making the challenge bigger than my God. It seemed like this mountain was just too big an obstacle for me to climb. Then as time passed, I came to realize that God wasn't calling me to produce some complex volume but simply to share my story and that of my parents.

God wants to use our stories to provide encouragement to others and to show them His faithfulness. If God called me to do something, I knew He was quite capable of equipping me. Still, I dragged my feet and did not move along with God's request.

But God had His own ways of propelling me toward His plan. At a Fourth of July celebration dinner in 2016, a Sunday school teacher from a church I was attending asked me to share about the freedom my family had experienced through immigrating from our homeland of Taiwan to the United States. With some hesitation, I agreed and wrote out our family's experiences. After I shared them at this event, many of those in attendance again encouraged me to write a book.

Time passed. Once again, I focused on my own limitations instead of focusing on how big and amazing is my God. Then in 2018, I traveled to Taiwan to visit my parents, who had moved back to their homeland. While I was there, Dad told me he was writing a book about his life in Mandarin, the national language of Taiwan. To me, this was another confirmation from God that I too was called to write my story. God showed me that even in my doubt and short sightedness, He orchestrates His ultimate plan and brings it to fruition.

But over a year later, I was still taking my time. In August 2019, I watched the movie *Little Women* and was inspired by the main character Jo, who dreamed of being a writer but didn't find success until she was encouraged to stop writing pulp fiction and write instead her own family's far more authentic and compelling story. God used that movie and other examples of authorship I kept bumping up against to encourage me to write my own story.

So in October 2019, I attempted once again to begin writing this book. A few weeks later, I read a Christian author's biographical account. In recounting his true life experiences, the author stated that he was not a writer by trade. This statement jumped out at me because he had in fact written the book I was holding in my hands and reading. At that moment, the Holy Spirit encouraged me that if God had helped this author write his life story, He could do the same for me.

March 2020 marked the beginning of the global COVID-19 pandemic. At that time, the Sunday school class I was attending was studying various key Bible characters like Abraham, Noah, and others. The common element between these faith "giants" was that God had asked each of them to do something that required their willingness to follow Him in obedience despite many unknowns, trusting that He would take care of the rest.

One character we studied that month was the apostle John, who was living in exile on the island of Patmos for his faithfulness in preaching the gospel. During John's exile, God called the apostle to write a book (Revelation 1:9-11), which of course became the final book of the New Testament. God bringing this passage up in class right at this time was another confirmation that He was calling me to write a book as well.

In November 2020, I had a dream in which God indicated specific individuals from my Sunday School class whom God had chosen to assist me in birthing this book so that He could use its story and message to encourage others. I felt timid about approaching these individuals. But when I did, they were all willing to help.

God has been so patient with me! One confirmation after another, and now here I am finally ready to write this book. All this time, I'd been telling myself something different than what God was directing me to do. I'd hesitated to take that first step, focusing instead on my fears until my fears became my personal Mount Himalaya, a huge, impassable mountain range rising in front of my path and stopping me dead in my tracks. This obstacle I'd allowed to dominate my mind had kept me from taking my next step toward God's plan for my life.

Have you ever doubted your abilities for the task God has in mind for you? If you are at all like me, you may have missed an opportunity because you were too immobilized by fear, uncertainty, or insecurity. Maybe your worries have kept you from trusting God to provide you with the means to overcome these uncertainties or fears.

A lot of our fights are in the spiritual world. Satan keeps us "circling the wagon" without progress. He has ways of blocking us from our destiny by paralyzing us in our thoughts, keeping us from stepping forward in faith. Satan will keep us in his trap as long as we allow him to keep us in doubt. As he did with Moses, he gets us to question God (Exodus 3-4). Will God provide, we ask ourselves, or will God let me fall flat on my face?

God reminded me that Jesus has already overcome Satan through His redemptive work on the cross. So I can let go of my fears to freefall into His arms. God didn't call me to write a book just to display the inadequacy of my English or writing skills but to use me for His glory. If He has called me, God will also provide me with the necessary means and skills to walk the path He has chosen for me.

God also reminded me of all the inadequacies Moses, Samson, Peter, and so many other biblical personages displayed. Yet God used them to do great and mighty things for His glory. He even used a donkey once to achieve His plan (Numbers 22:21-39). Now that is amazing!

God has been reaching for me and loving me unconditionally throughout my life. He has created me beautifully and molded me according to His plan. He has so faithfully encouraged me and guided me with the Holy Spirit's gentle whispers to my heart at different points of my life.

But my spiritual eyes couldn't always see that. I was too focused on my hurts. Though I occasionally reached forward to receive Him, I was too often sidetracked with life distractions.

Thankfully, God has so patiently waited for me to respond. He has repeatedly reminded me that I only need to be willing. He has everything else handled and in place for me to step into His plan. I've often requested that God show me all the details before I agree to proceed. I've had the nerve to actually bargain with God, saying, "If you will show me all the steps, God, then I will follow and obey."

But God doesn't work the way our world works, and God's logic is vastly different than human logic, as He pointed out to the prophet Isaiah.

> "For my thoughts are not your thoughts, neither are your ways my ways," declares the Lord.
>
> —Isaiah 55:8 NIV

Instead of revealing the entire road ahead, God provides us with enough light to get us safely to the next step so that we can continue leaning on Him as King David reminds us from his own experience.

> The LORD directs the steps of the godly. He delights in every details of their lives. Though they stumble, they will never fall, for the LORD holds them by the hand.
>
> —Psalm 37:23-24, NLT

In our human logic, we want to see the big picture and the little details of the entire plan. But if we ever saw the whole picture, we would run away because it would be too overwhelming. God's logic calls for us to trust that His plan for our lives has our best interests in mind. He is our Provider. He is there to guide us to each next step.

Eventually, we will look back and see clearly God's entire plan. This may not be until we are in heaven. In my own life, I can see how God has been moving me out of my comfort zone, that place where I need to know all the details. Since my profession is that of an engineer, this trait has served me well. God has wired me a certain way. But I've had to learn to take baby steps in trusting Him. I have to avoid the paralyzing trap of constantly assessing all the chances of possible failure. The engineering side of me dominates when it comes to risk assessment. It is a hazard of my profession that at times spills over into my walk with God.

When it does, God reminds me that joining Him in His plan is a cooperative partnership that is dependent on my willing heart and not on my abilities. He will equip for the journey and provide me the necessary resources as I lean on Him.

So here we go. Stepping forward and leaning on my Rock, Jesus my Savior, who is perfect in every way, I yield to His authority in heaven. He sacrificed Himself for my sins, so I am saved, loved, and cherished. I have a story to share with you, and my prayer is that it will glorify Him.

ONE

信望愛

THE CHI FAMILY JOURNEY

I magine walking around a strange place with your eyes closed. Are you able to take confident steps? Are you uncertain about the next step? Are you afraid you'll bump into something or maybe hurt yourself?

I've just asked you to step into an uncomfortable place so that you can better understand my parents. How will this help you? Well, because both my mom and dad are blind. Yes, you heard me right. Let me tell you their story and how their challenging journey helped me in turn walk through receiving and embracing God's unconditional love for me.

My dad's family name is Chi. His English-language name is Jim. His Asian given name is Chin-Chih, meaning "pond of gold" (金池). One of five children, Dad was born in 1944 in Taipei, the capital of Taiwan, an island nation off the coast of mainland

China. Taiwan was ceded to Japanese control in 1895. The island was a major Japanese base during WWII. After the Allied defeat of Japan in 1945, Taiwan was ceded back to the Republic of China under the rule of Generalissimo Chiang Kai-shek.

Today, the industrious, prosperous island of Taiwan, especially its capital Taipei, is not dissimilar to the bustling affluence of New York City. But in the aftermath of WWII, life was very difficult in Taiwan. My grandparents were extremely poor and unable to access healthcare. In 1947 when my dad was three years old, he contracted chickenpox. A very high fever burned out the nerves of his eyes, causing him to permanently lose his eyesight.

In the 1940s, Taiwan had no educational opportunities for the blind. Nor did they receive any financial assistance from government programs. The situation was exacerbated by the Chinese Civil War between the Republic of China nationalist government of Generalissimo Chiang Kai-shek and the Chinese Communist Party, led by CCP Chairman Mao Zedong. When Communist forces defeated ROC forces in December 1949, Chiang Kai-shek moved his government to Taiwan, making Taipei his new capital.

Along with ROC government forces, more than two million Chinese refugees also fled to Taiwan. This influx of refugees created extreme challenges for those already living in Taiwan, including hyperinflation (a highly accelerated inflation rate), which meant that the Taiwan currency quickly lost its value. The ROC regime also placed Taiwan under martial law, which lasted until the late 1980s with Chiang Kai-shek himself ruling until his death in 1975.

In the Taiwanese culture, the blind are considered "defective." In the 1940s and 50s when my dad was growing up, a blind person was either provided for by their family or they had no other recourse but to beg on the street. Also, even mandatory primary school education wasn't free, and any child with two parents didn't qualify for low-income assistance even if both parents were earning below the poverty level.

Neither of my dad's parents had any education, and both of their incomes were below the poverty level. But because he had two parents, Dad fell into this category. Since he couldn't get low-income assistance and his parents couldn't afford to pay the fees, he didn't attend school. Still, Dad didn't give up. Even at such a young age, he set himself to learn English on his own through listening to English-language radio.

My grandparents were Buddhist by cultural heritage but had no particular religious beliefs. Whether because of culture or temperament, neither of them expressed overt affection such as hugs or kisses toward each other or my dad. Nor did they ever speak of spiritual or emotional thoughts and feelings. So while my dad was provided with a roof over his head, what food they could afford, and basic clothing and footwear, his home environment was one of emotional neglect.

Thankfully, God blessed my dad with a benefactor, Dr. Wu Fu Chen (1918-1997), a Taiwanese ophthalmologist who was also a committed Christian. Dr. Chen's given name Wu Fu means "five happiness" (五福). Like his name, he was committed to the principle that the more you share happiness, the better the world will be. Dr. Chen donated a large percentage of the income from his medical practice to open a school to help the blind and teach them to be self-sufficient. Established in 1959, Mu-Kuang Learning Center for the Blind, now called Mu-Kuang Rehabilitation Center for the Blind, is still providing academic and professional training for the seeing-impaired in Yilan, Taiwan, not far from the capital, Taipei.

Dr. Chen provided my dad free room, board, and education for five years at the Mu-Kuang Learning Center for the Blind while Dad learned self-sufficiency skills. The facility taught Christian principles, Braille, which is a tactile alphabet that can read by touch, English language, basic life skills, and massage therapy, a professional skill the visually challenged could perform as an occupation.

Dr. Chen also sang hymns and shared the gospel with the students. His loving care and compassion toward my dad touched Dad's heart, helping him comprehend a divine love he'd never experienced from my grandparents. When he was eighteen years old, Dad accepted Jesus Christ as his Savior.

Dr. Chen's selfless dedication to the blind inspired in my dad the desire to pay forward the kindness he'd received to others who were visually challenged and in need. also wanted to study to become a pastor so he could share the gospel and help others. Recognizing my dad's potential, Dr. Chen spoke to the principal of Taiwan Theological College and Seminary about the possibility of enrolling Dad. The principal informed him that Dad would have to pass extremely difficult comprehensive English tests to enroll. But if he passed the tests, he would receive free tuition.

Dad studied hard and passed the English tests, which allowed him to enroll in the seminary. But even with free tuition, other expenses remained. Dr. Chen blessed Dad with funds for meals. Another Christian donor funded his book costs, and he received a scholarship to pay for other school expenses. Once he began his studies, Dad quickly realized that learning Hebrew and Latin would be necessary to become a pastor. Since there was no Braille available in Hebrew or Latin, he switched to a Christian Education major.

Part of Dad's studies included training at the MacKay Memorial Hospital, which was associated with George Leslie MacKay, the first Canadian Presbyterian missionary to preach the gospel to the people of Taiwan. This training included preaching the gospel to patients and hospital staff twice a day.

He would also accompany a pastor on visiting rounds to comfort and encourage patients and their families.

Throughout his life, Dad has never thought of his blindness as a handicap nor ever used it as an excuse. He has always had the mindset that God created him whole despite his blindness. He's always known that he was as capable as anyone else and had all the necessary tools for success.

He has also always been very persistent and bold. As a young man, he had a strong desire to go to the United States, a dream he eventually realized. Around 1964 when he was about twenty years old, he decided to write a letter to Lyndon B. Johnson, who was the American president at that time, expressing his dream of coming to the United States. He was delighted to receive a letter back encouraging him to diligently learn English and the necessary skills that would provide him with self-sufficiency. Taking this advice, Dad learned English well. He also mastered massage therapy and became a massage therapy instructor in Taipei.

In contrast to my dad, my mom had full sight during her growing up years. Her English-language name is Alice Wu Chi while her Asian given name is Chun-Chu, meaning "spring chrysanthemum" (春菊). Her family name is Wu. The oldest of four children, she was born in 1942 in Tainan, a city on the southeast coast of Taiwan almost the full length of the island from the capital of Taipei. Like my dad, she was raised in a family that was Buddhist by cultural heritage but non-practicing in any religious sense.

Mom was blessed to be able to attend school. At that time, primary school education went through sixth grade, followed by junior high and high school. Mom graduated from junior high, but she was not able to attend high school. Because her father owned property, she was not eligible to receive scholarships. But with three younger children to support, her parents couldn't afford to pay out-of-pocket for the higher costs of high school education.

Leaving school, Mom found a job at a ticket counter for a bus station, where she worked for several years. By the time she matured into a young lady in her early twenties, Taiwan's economy had begun to change. This was now the early 1960s. Taiwan had received $1.5 billion in economic aid and $2.4 billion in military assistance from the United States. The island's economy was shifting from mostly agriculture to light industry and various small and medium-sized business enterprises. Taiwan also began manufacturing many types of products for domestic consumption and export.

The summer she turned twenty, Mom contracted meningitis, a life-threatening bacterial infection that attacks the brain and spinal cord and can potentially lead to death within twenty-four hours. The meningitis affected Mom's nervous system so that she become legally blind and paralyzed. Though she didn't lose all sight like my dad, her eyesight was so bad she couldn't see details even five feet away, and glasses couldn't correct the issue.

One blessing was that she was able to receive healthcare. Additionally, her mother, sisters, and brother were able to help her in her recovery. Mom spent four and half months in a hospital in Kaohsiung, a large coastal city south of Tainan, where she received western-style medical treatments. During the first months, she was unable to chew, so she received only liquid meals. She was given so many shots that she ran out of skin surface.

After the first month, she learned to sit up again. In another month or so, she started relearning to walk. When she finally left the hospital, Mom was still very weak. She returned home to Tainan, where she did daily rehab with the help of my grandmother, uncle, and aunts. It took many years for her to fully regain her strength and heal as much as was possible.

God blessed Mom in that she was able to regain some of her eyesight and walk again. Many of the doctors and nurses said she was lucky to be alive, much less recover some sight and mobility. While the western medical treatments had saved her life, she also continued many years of eastern herbal medical treatments, which helped her body heal from the toxicity of the western medications.

When Mom was twenty-two year old, she went to the Taipei Commission for the Blind, where she started two years of switchboard operator training. My parents met shortly after she finished her training in 1966. Mom was now working at the Mackay Memorial Hospital in Taipei as a phone switchboard operator, connecting outside calls to the patients staying at the hospital.

Meanwhile, Dad was finishing up his seminary training, which included visiting the hospital to encourage and comfort patients and their families. He'd heard that a young woman who was legally blind was working there as a switchboard operator. Curious about her story, he contacted her. They began talking on a regular basis. Dad gravitated toward my mom's persistence and strong spirit. Mom gravitated toward his servant's heart and wanted to help him.

They started dating. While Mom was still a non-practicing Buddhist, she'd been exposed to Christian influence and teachings through her work at the hospital. After asking Dad a lot of questions about his faith, she began attending church with him. Many years later, she shared with me that her Christian faith was at first more about attending church, but she came to recognize that God had been there with her even in the hardest trials and to be grateful for God's loving care even before she knew who He was as heavenly Father.

My parents continued their courtship for a couple of years. Dad eventually had to drop out of his seminary studies to support my grandparents. He taught my mom massage therapy. He also went to the Massage Labor Department to get further training and be fully licensed as a professional massage therapist. My parents' goal was to get married and start a joint massage therapy business to support themselves as well as help support my grandparents.

Both sides of their families expressed a lot of concern and opposition over the possibility of their marriage. Since both of my parents were legally blind, the families were uncertain how they would take care of themselves, much less any future children. From their point of view, both families felt that my mom and dad would need to rely on other people to take care of them rather than having any possibility of independence as a married couple.

But God had a plan for my parents. Through their persistence, they were eventually able to calm the concerns of their families and overcome their challenges. In the end, Mom and Dad received the support and blessings they needed from both sides of the family. They were married on December 10, 1969.

TWO

信望愛

GOD'S PLAN FOR
THE CHI FAMILY

D r. Wu Fu Chen had inspired my dad with his devotion to the blind. Dad also wanted to model his life after the way both his benefactor and the apostle Paul in the New Testament had helped others and preached the gospel while maintaining a professional career to provide financially for themselves. Dr. Chen had built up a busy ophthalmology practice to support his family as well as the school for the blind. The apostle Paul had been a tentmaker and church-planting missionary at the same time (Acts 18:1-4).

Dad's vision was to establish a school in Taipei to help the blind. So he decided that he and Mom would work at night as massage therapists to provide for themselves, then fundraise for the school during the day. For many years, my parents worked at night until 2 a.m. at the international tourist hotel as massage therapists, then devoted the daytime hours to starting the school. Almost every weekend, they shared in various churches about their vision as well as speaking with other charity organizations. They also devoted countless hours working with volunteers to write fund-raising letters to churches too far away to visit personally. They sought governmental funding as well, but little was available for the blind or other disabilities.

While this involved an enormous amount of hard work, my parents were successful. On June 21, 1975, the Taipei Benevolent Educational Society for the Blind opened its doors. Much like the Mu-Kuang Learning Center for the Blind where my dad attended in Yilan, the Educational Society teaches skills necessary for the visually impaired to be self-sufficient, including basic life skills, English, and massage therapy.

My parents continued their own massage therapy practice while teaching at the new facility. They also continued fundraising to cover rent for the location and salaries for supplementary teachers. Their long-term vision was for the Educational Society to own its facility rather than continuing to pay rent. This was no small task to accomplish since real estate in Taiwan is very expensive. But God blessed my parents' fundraising efforts with sufficient support to purchase the entire fourth floor of a commercial building in Taipei.

By this time, my parents were raising three small children along with balancing their massage therapy jobs and the school. I was the firstborn, entering my parents' lives in 1970. My Asian name is Wen Hui (文慧). In sixth grade, my English tutor gave me the name Wendy as my English-language name. Since Wendy is pretty close to my Asian name of Wen Hui, it was easy for me and others to remember. A year later, my first brother was born. His English name is Jeff, and his Asian Name is Chien-Feng (建鋒). My second brother George was born in 1976. His Asian name is Rong Chon (榮聰).

Balancing two careers and three children would have been difficult to juggle even for parents with eyesight. My grandparents helped where they could with childcare and my parents' work. When my brothers and I were infants, baby sitters cared for us during the late night shifts my parents worked at the hotel. During daytime hours, they were very busy with the Educational Society. In consequence, I don't recall ever spending much time with my parents.

Looking back, I know this wasn't easy for my mom as she wanted to be there for my brothers and me but also to support my dad. But she rarely spoke of such struggles, always endeavoring to maintain a strong, steady presence for my dad and her children.

Once the fourth floor facility had been acquired for the Educational Society, my parents were able to live free of charge in a small efficiency apartment about six hundred square feet in back of the classroom area. Since Dad was now the main support of his own parents, my paternal grandparents along with one of my uncles moved into the apartment as well.

Though apartment is perhaps stretching reality. My parents and all three kids slept in the apartment's single room. My grandparents and uncle slept on a wooden platform my grandfather had built in the open area where classes were held. While cramped quarters for five adults and three children, this free living space was a big blessing since any housing in Taiwan is very expensive.

With a limited income and eight people to feed, we ate very simply with meals typically consisting of rice, vegetables, and fruits. For protein, we supplemented this diet with eggs, chicken, and sometimes fish. Only rarely did we eat other meats, and fancy cakes or pastry desserts were for even rarer celebratory occasions. While I wasn't aware of it as a small child, this forced simplicity of diet was a very wholesome way of eating that in the long run fostered an overall healthy lifestyle for our entire family and which I've chosen for my own health to carry into my adult life.

Despite the challenges, some things about life in Taipei were good. The city had many modes of transportation. My parents took the convenient, inexpensive city buses, taxis, or a motorcycle service to get around. The motorcycle service was the most convenient as they could call or reserve a pickup time. The motorcycle driver would then pick them up and take them where they wanted just like a taxi but far more inexpensively. The motorcycles could also access the many narrow alleys for which Taipei's development layout was famous where taxis wouldn't fit. My parents used taxis only when it was raining hard and they didn't want to arrive at their destination soaked through.

My grandfather didn't like riding buses or taxis, so he would ride his bicycle instead. On larger boulevards, bicycles and motorbikes might have dedicated lanes while cars and buses share lanes. But when it comes to smaller streets, bicycle, motorbikes, scooters, cars, and buses all share the common lanes. Maneuvering safely through this congestion takes skill and experience and can be nerve-wrecking if you aren't used to it.

My grandmother experienced motion sickness any time she was in a vehicle, so she walked everywhere she went. Since the Educational Society was on the fourth floor and there was no elevator, we all climbed up and down four flights of stairs many times a day. All this exercise kept us in excellent health, including my aging grandparents. Sometimes a lack of conveniences in life can be a blessing.

With three young children in the home, one advantage of having my grandparents sharing our small living space was that they could now give more time to caring for us while my parents devoted themselves to their massage practice and dream of providing resources for the blind. Since this kept my parents very busy, I spent a lot of time with my grandparents. My grandmother, whom I called *āmā*, the Taiwanese term for Grandma, was not talkative or affectionate but very serious and stoic. In contrast, my grandfather, whom I called *a-gong* (阿公), the Taiwanese term for Grandpa, always had time for me and made me feel like I mattered the world to him.

A-gong was a doer and very dexterous with his hands. He crafted many items for the non-profit library, including floor-to-ceiling sturdy metal bookshelves to hold the heavy braille books. Because he had little education, he couldn't get a good-paying office job. But he and my uncle ran a nighttime market game prize booth where customers purchased tickets that opened up like a fortune cookie, revealing prize winnings that ranged from candy, nice pencils, little cheap toys, jump ropes, pretty journal books, glow-in-the-dark laser guns, little toy helicopters, and pet mice or pigeons.

These earnings helped supplement my parents' massage income. A-gong also helped my dad run errands and do basic chores around the Educational Society. My uncle spent his own days on the streets, smoking and drinking. A kindly, smiling person, he was physically powerful but had mental challenges and experienced seizures, a reason he wasn't able to support himself independently. I was still in elementary school when he was hit by a train while walking along a train rail and instantly killed.

When not working A-gong enjoyed spending quality time with others, especially having teatime with them. The only tea he would drink was oolong tea, a traditional Chinese semi-dark tea that is high in antioxidants and other health benefits. My personal quality time with A-gong included going on errands with him on his bicycle, after which he would treat me to shaved ice with yummy toppings like sweet red adzuki beans, green mung beans, chewy tapioca pearls and mochi rice balls, all drizzled with lots of sweetened condensed milk.

But enjoying a cold, sweet treat together wasn't what I considered important about our outings. A-gong always made clear how much he treasured these moments with me by not rushing through them but focusing all his attention on our time together. We laughed together and had fun with the simplest things in life. I remember when I was quite small playing with his big earlobes and rubbing his military haircut.

And I too would engage all my attention with A-gong. He taught me to show my love to others through spending quality time with the purpose of intimately and genuinely loving them at that moment. Thanks to A-gong, I grew up focusing on relationships and friendships instead of material things. We had few physical possessions as a family. Looking back, I realize this was a blessing in disguise.

At that time, Taiwan's educational system was free up to ninth grade, though as with my dad and his siblings, the cost of books, supplies, and other fees could still make attendance difficult. Students were responsible for doing the chores of cleaning the school before and after classes. My brothers and I had to walk to school since none of my family members owned a car or even drove. This meant we had to leave quite early in the morning for school and returned fairly late after helping with school cleaning.

Outside of school, I spent most of my time doing homework. I would also make my own paper dolls and paper doll dresses since my parents couldn't afford to buy me real dolls. Sometimes, my brothers and I would play on the four flights of stairs using the rock, paper, scissors game to advance up and down the stairs. An occasional piece of candy was considered a major treat. My youngest brother George was a homebody and liked to play at home. But Jeff enjoyed playing at the park and walking around the neighborhoods by himself.

During these growing up years, my brothers and I didn't have a close relationship with my parents since they were too busy to spend quality time with us. Nor did they show much physical affection to each other or us. This wasn't unusual as it was part of Chinese culture, and they'd been raised this way by their own parents, but it was still hurtful to me. Looking back, I recognize how hard they were working to support a household of eight as well as their non-profit for the blind.

The relationship between my dad and A-gong was not a close one. Though A-gong was very loving towards me and had a tender heart, he had a temper and was easily angered. He was also not happy about my father's conversion to Christianity. While he'd help my dad in a heartbeat if there was need, he never showed his son any open affection. And my dad didn't show his father affection either. This was simply how they'd both been raised, but it made me sad, especially since I never understood why A-gong could be so nice to me but get so angry at others.

My parents too didn't teach us healthy conflict resolution skills. Though they had faith in God and trusted God to bring them through these challenging times, they were both strong-minded with very different opinions and often resorted to shouting matches as a way to handle personal conflict. This bothered me a lot when I was little, and I learned to avoid anything that would create conflict. Sitting around talking about our day or our feelings or openly discussing issues as a family just wasn't done. Instead, I internalized everything that bothered me. To keep my mind on more pleasant things, I spent a lot of time with A-gong, anime books, and one close friend in my later elementary school years while keeping my thoughts to myself.

In short, there wasn't much harmony in our household, and neither my brothers nor I learned healthy conflict resolution or had good communication with my grandma, parents, uncle, and siblings during my childhood and growing-up years.

THREE

信望愛

A MAN OF MANY DREAMS

B y the 1970s, Taiwan had been under martial law and the
sole dictatorship of Generalissimo Chiang Kai-shek for a
quarter-century. In 1971, Taiwan lost its UN seat, which the island
had held since the Republic of China (ROC) regime had moved its
capital from mainland China to Taiwan in 1949. China had been
one of the original member states of the United Nations, founded
in 1945, when mainland China was still under ROC rule.

Both the ROC and the Chinese Communist Party (CCP)
claimed to be the only legitimate government of China, which
encompassed the mainland, the island of Taiwan, and some
smaller islands. So both claimed China's single UN seat. But a
hotly-contested UN resolution in October 1971 awarded the
seat to the People's Republic of China as China's sole

representative in the United Nations, a situation that has remained a political controversy to the present day.

Then in 1973, a global oil crisis caused a worldwide panic when the Organization of Arab Petroleum Exporting Countries (OAPEC) declared an oil embargo against the United States and other nations that had supported Israel during the Yom Kippur War. All these events adversely affected Taiwan's economy. Work was hard to find, especially for the blind, and wages were low with much poverty and great disparity of incomes.

My dad had dreamed of going to the United States since he'd written that long-ago letter to President Lyndon B. Johnson. Now he had even greater reason to go as he longed to give his family a better future. With three small children ranging at that time from newborn to age six, there was no way he could take his entire family. But in 1976, he finally made plans to travel to the United States to do a one-year rehabilitation training program at the Arkansas Enterprise for the Blind.

Dad's first trip was a challenge from the very beginning. A taxi took our entire family to the airport in Taipei to see my dad off on his flight to the United States. Once we'd climbed out of the taxi, the taxi driver took off with all my dad's luggage except for a few changes of clothing in a carry-on bag Dad had fortunately already removed from the taxi. This setback did not stop my dad. Trusting God to take care of him, he boarded the plane anyway.

Even after arriving in the United States, Dad faced many challenges. But God sent many helpers and assistants. God was providing for my dad one step at a time. One challenge was that he had to translate every word in every textbook into braille since there were no braille books available for him to study. God provided some amazing friends who spent many late nights reading textbooks and other study materials to him while he wrote down their words in braille. Dad was very grateful for their help.

Another amazing provision of God took place shortly before the end of his one-year study program. Dad wanted to learn American massage techniques and compare them to the oriental acupressure massage he'd learned in Taiwan. He started calling various massage facilities to locate an expert massage teacher. A masseur at one of the massage facilities recommended an excellent trainer named John T. Brown who taught at the YMCA massage school in Fort Worth, Texas. Dad was scheduled to fly back to Taiwan in less than a week, but he wanted to meet with Mr. Brown before leaving the United States. So he bought an airplane ticket to Fort Worth on faith that Mr. Brown would be available to speak with him when he arrived.

But God had a different plan for my dad. Before heading to the airport for his flight to Fort Worth, Dad stopped by a Chinese restaurant for a meal. There he met a professor of physics named Dr. Young, who was also having a meal at the restaurant.

Curious about this clearly blind Asian man who had come in alone to eat, Dr. Young struck up a conversation with my dad. He was fascinated to discover that as a blind person Dad had come on his own all the way from Taiwan to study in Arkansas.

As they talked, Dr. Young learned that my dad was flying that day to Fort Worth to meet Mr. Brown. He told Dad that his flight would likely be cancelled due to a big snowstorm that was blowing in. Could my dad change his flight to another day?

Dad explained that he couldn't change to a later flight because he was leaving the United States in just a few days. Nor did he want to lose this opportunity to speak with Mr. Brown as he might not be able to come back to the United States. Dr. Young very kindly offered to drive my dad from Arkansas to Fort Worth so he wouldn't miss meeting Mr. Brown. The trip took them eight hours driving through a worsening snowstorm, but they made it safely to Fort Worth.

When they arrived at the Fort Worth YMCA, Mr. Brown proved available and willing to meet with my dad. At that time, Mr. Brown had a painful hip problem, so Dad offered to massage him. Mr. Brown agreed. He was both pleased and surprised when Dad's massage relieved his pain. He asked my dad what type of massage technique he'd used.

Dad went on to show Mr. Brown the acupressure massage techniques he'd learned in Taiwan. Mr. Brown wanted Dad to stay and teach those techniques at the Fort Worth massage school. Of course Dad couldn't stay since he was scheduled to fly back to Taiwan in just a few days. But Mr. Brown assured him he'd find some way to bring my dad back.

It was because of this trip with Dr. Young sacrificing his time to drive my dad to meet Mr. Brown and Mr. Brown's persistence and willingness to sponsor my parents through the American special skills visa program that my family was eventually able to come to the United States. This was a divine appointment only God could have arranged between Dr. Young, Mr. Brown, and my dad. Dad was so thankful for God's direct intervention in his life that would prove so crucial to changing the life course of our entire family.

After Dad returned to Taiwan, his experiences in the United States motivated him to continue his non-profit school for the blind while waiting for Mr. Brown's sponsorship. Around 1979, Dad created the Talking Books Library for the Blind in Taipei. This was the first library for the blind in all of Taiwan, and it provided audiobooks on cassette tapes as well as braille books and other resources for the blind that would broaden their quality of life. It even had a recording studio to produce the audiotapes.

FOUR

信望愛

FREEDOM AT ALL COST

Has anyone ever thought you were crazy for doing something that in their mind was too big a risk and made no logical sense? Yet even though the logic didn't add up, you knew it was the right choice and that God had already paved your way when you couldn't even visualize the path of possibility. It reminds me of the promise God gave the prophet Isaiah for his people Israel, which still remains true for us today.

> See, I am doing a new thing! Now it springs up; do you not perceive it? I am making a way in the wilderness and streams in the wasteland.
>
> —Isaiah 43:19 NIV

My dad still had a strong desire to return to the United States to provide better opportunities for his family. In 1979 when I was around nine years old, my parents finally received the travel and work permits Mr. Brown had been working on through a skilled workers visa program sponsored by the YMCA in Ponca City, Oklahoma. So my parents, younger brothers, and I left Taiwan to live in Ponca City.

My grandparents thought my parents were crazy. Our family at the time consisted of two blind parents and three kids ranging in age from nine years old down to two years old. My father had learned passable English through his studies, but my mom, brothers Jeff and George, and I knew only very basic English. Moving from Taiwan's capital of Taipei, a metropolitan area of several million people, to Ponca City, Oklahoma, with a population of less than 25,000 was a major culture shock. The ethnic demography was overwhelmingly Caucasian with small minorities of Native American, Hispanic, and African-American but no Asian community.

To complicate matters, there was no easy access to public transit such as we'd had in Taiwan or even existed in New York City. This made mobility very limited if you didn't own a car or drive. Thankfully, we did receive various types of help from church members, including people who kindly volunteered to drive us places as needed.

This included attending church every Sunday, a non negotiable for my parents. I didn't enjoy going and complained often. I didn't want to participate in any church youth activities or Sunday school as my English was poor and I didn't feel as though I fit in. I just wanted to come home as soon as church was over.

In short, I didn't transition to America at all well. The environment, culture, language, even the food were all so different from what I knew. I was overjoyed when just a year later we had to return to Taiwan due to some visa paperwork. I was very content to be back with my grandfather and all the things I was familiar with and loved. As you can tell by now, I am not fond of changes.

But after working in Taipei with the two non-profits—the Society for the Blind and Talking Books Library—for just a few years, Dad felt a strong leading to head back to the United States to pursue a better future for our family. As always, Mom followed his lead. So we geared up again to return to the United States. On July 12, 1984, we received permanent residency status to move to the United States. I was now fourteen years old, my brother Jeff thirteen, and my youngest brother George nine.

This time my parents got massage therapist positions at the YMCA in Corsicana, Texas, a town similar in size to Ponca City though with a larger mix of non-Caucasian minorities, including almost one-third Hispanic and twenty percent African-American. But there was still no Asian community nearby, and adjustment to a strange country was even harder than the last trip since we kids were older now.

We found a rental house just across the street from YMCA, so my parents were able to walk across the street to go to work. My brothers and I took a school bus to get to the local school. As soon as we'd settled in, Dad contacted a nearby Baptist church. They kindly provided us with transportation to church and the grocery store. Some of my parents' YMCA massage clients also helped at times with transportation.

Transition for my brothers and me into the public school system was also much harder this time since we had to enter into higher grades. Our English was barely first grade level, and there were no ESL (English as a Second Language) classes, though the school did provide some tutoring. I was placed straight into seventh grade and had no idea what the teachers were saying.

Each evening, my brothers and I would look up words from our English, history, and science classes in the dictionary, studying until very late at night. Many nights I went to bed in tears because I was struggling so much in school. The only class subject where I excelled was math except for word problems since the math I'd studied in Taiwan was far more advanced than what I was learning in the United States. It was at least a couple years before I had to learn anything new in that class.

We continue to struggle financially as well. A couple years later, we moved from Corsicana to Dallas, Texas, a much larger city of more than a million, where my mom found a massage therapist job at a four-star hotel in downtown Dallas. This job provided a much better income for our family. The city's public transport system also had an excellent handicapped rider assistance program that made getting around much easier. Mom was very grateful for God's provision in this way.

Dad also found massage work at the same hotel for a while until he had to fly back to Taiwan to deal with some issues with the Educational Society non-profit. Another blessing of our move to Dallas was that my parents found a Taiwanese church to attend. Church members also volunteered with transportation and helped us get into a Section 8 government housing apartment.

Despite all the difficulties and challenges, my parents were determined this time around to make the United States our permanent home. Dad's dream had always been to come to the United States. He recognized the United States as a Promised Land of new opportunities. He desired a better life for his family. Economic and educational opportunities remained quite limited for the lower classes in Taiwan such as my dad's family had been, and good career choices were scarce for the blind and women.

More than that, my parents wanted to raise their family in freedom. Since the 1980s, Taiwan has made great strides towards a working democracy, so some readers may wonder why I would even bring up the topic of freedom. But at the time my parents were working toward coming to the United States, Taiwan was still under martial law with thirty years of that martial law under the direct dictatorship of Chiang Kai-shek until his death in 1975. An unswerving desire for freedom and the opportunities the United States offers for success if someone is willing to work hard was what drove my parents to risk everything to come to the United States.

There are many things about the United States for which immigrants are grateful. Let me name just a few. To immigrants from countless different countries around the world, coming to the United States typically means the opportunity to:

- Create your own destiny provided that you have the drive and ambition.

- Be part of a society that is friendly to immigrants.

- Take advantage of economic/employment opportunities.

- Receive educational opportunities and financial assistance.

- Enjoy political and religious freedoms.

- Partake in the abundant resources available to the disabled.

- Be an adventurer, a wanderer, an opportunity seeker!

These are just a few benefits of living in a land of freedom. My family is grateful for the many benefits they have received from being in the United States. Beyond those listed above, here are some specific blessings for which we are thankful as a family.

- Supportive church family. Various church families were warm, caring, and generous with their love and help.

- Financial and housing assistance. With my parents' limited income, this financial assistance helped us through challenging periods.

- Big living spaces. After being accustomed to seven people living in a small efficiency apartment, we didn't know what to do with all the living area and backyard of our American homes. We'd always slept as a family in one room, so when we moved into our first YMCA housing with three large bedrooms, we pulled mattresses into the living-room to be together. It took a while before we became accustomed to sleeping in our own bedrooms.

- Good health care. The choices of medical expertise are good to have.

- Good traffic control and compliance with traffic rules. The orderly traffic compliance by most compared to the chaotic traffic in most of Taiwan creates a safe environment for the pedestrians and other drivers.

- Clean air. The excellent overall air quality in the United States compared to Taiwan and many other countries is a blessing for our lungs and body.

- Uninterrupted utility and water services. There were times in Taipei when we would need to fill the bathtub and any other available containers with water due to water shortages and interruptions.

- Educational opportunity. Being the first female in our family to go to college was a great blessing for me and my family.

- Self-sufficiency in transportation. Due to my parents' eyesight limitations, I had the opportunity to receive my driver's license at a very young age to drive my family places.

- Good career opportunity. Here in the United States, I had the freedom to choose a career in engineering such as would have been impossible in Taiwan. The field of engineering is a male-dominated field in both Taiwan and the U.S. Most of my college classmates were males, and I am still outnumbered by my male peers in the workplace. My brothers also enjoyed great career opportunities. Jeff has worked in oil, tech, and trucking industries. George, who had less difficulties in school since he was much younger when we moved, got his degree in the field of aerospace and works at NASA.

- Diversity. We have lived as a family in many diverse neighborhoods. As a result, we've learned to embrace people as people and not hold biases due to differing skin color or culture. Ponca City, OK, was mainly Caucasian, but the neighborhood to which we moved in Dallas, TX, was predominately African-American at the time. We then moved to North Dallas, which was largely Korean and Hispanic. I have made many friends from many different cultural and ethnic backgrounds. I never see them for their skin color but as individuals with unique personalities according to how God created us.

Despite the various challenges we've had to face, my family and I count ourselves so blessed to have this opportunity to be in the United States. During the winter of 1990, our entire family received U.S. citizenship. What a great blessing for the many future generations of our family. What a great gift my parents have worked toward to bless us with their vision and hard work in making this dream come true.

FIVE

信望愛

MY JOURNEY

Freedom has been defined as "the power or right to act, speak, or think as one wants without hindrance or restraint; democracy." But there is a second definition of freedom that comes to mind—freedom in the spiritual perspective, as the apostle Paul described it in his second epistle to the Corinthian church.

> Now the Lord is the Spirit, and where the Spirit of the Lord is, there is freedom.
>
> —2 Corinthians 3:17 NIV

So let me now share my own spiritual struggles and journey to spiritual freedom. My spiritual connection with God began when I was in elementary school. My family attended church regularly throughout my childhood in Taiwan and after we moved to the United States. But though I went to church with my parents all the way through my high school years, I was mainly going through the motions of a regular Sunday routine. I didn't develop a relationship with God through seeking God in His Word or leaning on Him during everyday challenges. I didn't even come close to knowing what it means to be in a relationship with God.

My lack of a close relationship with my parents was the basis of what and who I believed God to be—distant and almost nonexistent. When I was eight years old, my mom, brothers, and I were baptized together in a Presbyterian church. But my participation in this act was solely obeying my parents' wishes for the family rather than any personal commitment to God.

Also, while we attended church as a family, my parents didn't speak openly of their faith, and emphasis was far more on learning to be self-sufficient and working hard to meet needs and resolve problems rather than praying to the Holy Spirit for guidance or trusting God to supply. My parents always expressed gratitude for God's divine provision and all the godly church people who helped us. But there was also always a lot of worry and outbursts of anger when things weren't going well.

Looking back, I know that my parents were still baby Christians growing in their faith after having been raised in secular Buddhism. Life as two blind adults navigating through a strange culture while trying to raise and protect three children was a constant struggle. Since I can admit I still struggle in my faith all these years later even after having grown up in church, I now understand far better all they were going through. But I also grew up anxious, determined to be self-sufficient, and focused on fixing my own problems rather than trusting a heavenly Father to be there for me.

After we moved permanently to the United States, I was not at all grateful for the freedom and opportunities my parents had fought hard to provide for my brothers and me. I focused instead on what I missed. From my perspective, life in Taiwan had been great. I was content being with my grandfather and the single close friend I'd made in elementary school. A readily available transit system made it easy for our family to go wherever we wanted.

When we moved to the United States, we were suddenly living in small southern towns in Oklahoma and Texas where we couldn't get anywhere without a car. Also, we could barely communicate in English. How was this an advancement or better opportunity for our family compared to Taiwan?

At fourteen, I also had to grow up fast because my grandparents were no longer with us to help care for the household. My parents worked seven days a week to provide the bare essentials. So I had to be the third adult in the family and take care of my two younger brothers.

Also, in Taiwan the non-profit's secretary had been there to read email and documents to my parents. Now I had to be their eyes to go through all their documents, email, and even finances. I provided my arm for them to hold onto so they knew when to step up or down. When we were out and about, it was my responsibility to describe for them all that I saw. Instead of appreciating how hard they in turn were working to support their family, I felt I was being used as a tool or as their secretary most of the time.

In Taiwan, I'd had at least one good friend. As a teenager in the United States, I found friendship hard to come by. I was shy and had trouble communicating proficiently in English. I was always afraid of being laughed at if I pronounced a word incorrectly or used improper grammar. It was several years after our final move to the United States before I felt comfortable attending church youth group activities.

My academic difficulties were not improved by the high expectations my parents placed on me and the constant emphasis on making school my number one priority. Since I was the oldest child, my parents wanted to make sure I would graduate from college and excel in my future career. "Performance" was the driving force of my life at the time. My parents pushed me to achieve good grades, and there was zero room for failure. They often reminded me of how much they had sacrificed so we could receive a good education and opportunity. Critical comments were a constant in my life, and I didn't receive any loving encouragement to moderate the criticism.

Thankfully, by high school I had mastered fairly well both spoken and written English and was making straight As. But as time went on, I came to resent both my parents and God. Why were we even here in this strange country that felt so alien to me? I felt like I was in prison. I hadn't asked for any of this. My parents' decision to move to the United States had stolen my happiness. Assisting with their needs in exchange for food and shelter seemed to be the only basis of our relationship. Emotional and spiritual needs were left completely unmet.

My parents and I simply didn't know how to express our love to each other, and we didn't talk about things. This left a big hole inside of me. I ended up becoming depressed and at times very angry. I placed a lot of blame for this on my parents and was unable to see the benefits I now recognize that our move to the United States have provided me and my family.

Not far into my high school years, Dad moved back to Taiwan to deal with continuing problems at the Educational Society. When we'd come to the United States, he'd hired someone to manage the non-profit. But that person hadn't worked out well, so he had to return to take over. Mom stayed in the United States with my brothers and me.

By this time, we were in Dallas with access to a Taiwanese church and in a multi-cultural environment. During the rest of high school, I continued spending a lot of time studying and learning English and increasingly excelled academically. I also made several close friends who were also from other countries, two from Korea and another from Central America. They could relate to my struggles in the English language, and we helped each other at school.

While I continued to be a homebody and didn't socialize much, I did participate in Spanish club, Key Club, and National Honor Society activities. After school, I kept busy doing homework, preparing dinner, and keeping my youngest brother George company. Much younger than the rest of us when we moved to the U.S., George had learned English quickly and excelled academically. My brother Jeff, a year younger than me, took less interest in academics but like my grandfather was outstanding at making things and figuring things out. He was also athletic and spent a lot of time playing tennis after school.

On weekends, I drove Mom to and from her massage therapy appointments. We also continued attending the Taiwanese church on Sundays. We occasionally spoke on the phone with my dad and grandparents. But long distance to Taiwan was very expense, so we couldn't call often.

Then one night in my sophomore year of high school, I had a dream that my grandfather came to visit me. He smiled warmly at me and said, "I've come to say goodbye."

"Why are you saying goodbye?" I asked him. "We are about to go back to Taiwan to visit you."

A-gong didn't answer my question but just gave me a hug. Then with another warm smile, he again said, "Goodbye."

Then I woke up. I could hear my mom talking to someone on the phone. As I listened, I realized with horror that the conversation was about my grandfather and that he had just passed away. This was devastating to me. I was so depressed at the loss of my beloved A-gong. My mom and I flew back to Taiwan for my grandfather's funeral while my brothers stayed in Texas. It was the first time I'd seen my dad in a couple years, but I don't remember really speaking with him. Everyone was too busy with the funeral.

Dad never did return to the United States to live and visited only a few times, so my brothers and I saw very little of him over the next decades. Along with managing the non-profit, he did some nighttime massage therapy and taught massage therapy classes to support himself. Mom eventually moved back to Taiwan to help him once her children were all graduated from college and married. But during our teen years, she was the only financial support for our household, so we kids saw even less of her.

At this time, I was already not in a good place spiritually. Since my baptism back in Taiwan, I hadn't grown much spiritually since I'd done that mainly to please my dad. But now with this big loss of my A-gong, I felt even more resentment toward my parents and God for bringing me to the United States. I was unable to see God's blessing in my life, and I was so hurt in my heart that I couldn't see anything else good around me. There were times I just wanted to die, and I didn't understand why God wanted to keep me here on this planet and in this country.

As I progressed through high school, my depression lifted somewhat as I was starting to see the future benefits and possibilities for my life in the United States. This place of freedom could be as grand as my imagination and willingness to explore or as limited as my own limited view.

As I neared my senior year of high school, several teachers recognized my leadership potential, which I did not at the time. They encouraged me to run for officer positions in the various clubs in which I was involved. Other students must have seen the same potential as they ended up voting for me. During my senior year, I served as president of the Key Club and the Spanish Club.

Over my final years of high school, I also formed many friendships. My involvement in these clubs helped me to bloom as a person and become more extrovert. My senior year, I was voted among those graduates "Most Likely to Succeed." I finished high school with an unbroken four full years on the A honor roll. All those years of studying and hard work finally had its reward!

Six

信望愛

Spiritual Freedom

My journey toward spiritual freedom didn't begin until after I started college. When it came time to select a major in college, I still wasn't sure what I wanted to do. Since I was good with sciences and math, a friend of my parents suggested engineering. Their daughter was studying electrical engineering. After speaking to her and doing some research, I decided to try that field.

I began researching as well which college to attend. I felt a strong need to find myself and be my own person. I looked for colleges far enough that I could be independent but close enough I could drive home without getting too tired. I also wanted to be far enough away that my mom would lessen her dependency on me and depend more on my brothers and others.

I finally selected the University of Texas, located in Austin, the capital of Texas, about three hours from my family in Dallas.

My dad was in the United States for a visit when I left for college, and as I said goodbye, I hugged my parents for the very first time. I purposely hugged them because I wanted a better relationship with my parents and a better bonding for my future children and their children after them. This embrace was the first step for me to understand God's embrace.

Since my parents weren't in Austin to supervise my behavior, I no longer felt any compulsion to go to church every Sunday. But God had a very different plan. I'd never been away from home before, not even for a sleepover, and being away from home wasn't what I'd imagined it to be. I didn't enjoy being away from my family as I'd thought I would. Though I'd resented taking care of them, I now deeply missed my parents and my brothers.

I recognize now that I was missing what was familiar to me but also that I wasn't aware of the real bond I had with my family even if we experienced conflicts and resentment. Nor did I like the change of moving somewhere I didn't know people or my surroundings. This resistance to change was the reason I hadn't liked moving from Taiwan to the United States. But this time I'd moved voluntarily, and I'd done so just to get away from my parents. I guess this is one example of the common idiom that you need to be careful what you wish for!

During my freshman year, I lived on the University of Texas campus. Walking out of my dorm just two weeks into the school year, I noticed a church booth near the Student Union area among other organization booths. The booth represented a local Baptist church. When I stopped by the booth, the church members there were warm and welcoming. I accepted their invitation and began attending that church. God also blessed me with many Christian college friends as my new spiritual family.

A couple months later, I met a young man whom God used to develop my faith. We first met at an on-campus Asian dance party I was attending with some new friends. The young man was also a student at UT and was gentle-natured, loving, and patient in personality. He was also very enthusiastic about attending church, fellowshipping with other Christians, and being involved in church activities.

The young man invited me to visit his own church, which was also Baptist. I was greatly attracted by his kind, helping attitude toward others and his enthusiasm to be involved in church. When I visited his church, I met many warm, loving Asian Christians. During this same time, I was struggling in one of my physics classes, and he offered to help tutor me.

I began attending his church. After spending more time together at church and university, the young man asked if we could date. I was stunned. He could have dated any of the most beautiful girls I saw in church. Yet he saw me as worthy of being loved. He saw in me characteristics God was also able to see but that I couldn't. The lack of affection from my parents had influenced my own sense of self-worth to the point that I'd believed Satan's lies and convinced myself I couldn't be loved. It took me some time to accept that this friendship could be turning into something more. I will talk more about this relationship later.

Throughout that freshman year, God challenged my faith. I was attending church regularly. I also made a clear decision to accept Jesus Christ as my Lord and Savior, which I'd never done before even though I had believed in the existence of God and attended a Christian church most of my life.

But I still wasn't reading the Bible much other than opening it to verses the pastor was preaching on or passages we were studying in Sunday school. I was familiar with basic Bible stories and even knew Scripture passages that spoke of God's love. But I still had no heart understanding that God already loved me unconditionally since before I was even born so there was no point in trying to get my heavenly Father to love me through performance.

In Psalm 139, King David describes how intimately God knows us and how He is with us every step of the way.

> You have searched me, Lord, and you know me. You know when I sit and when I rise; you perceive my thoughts from afar. You discern my going out and my lying down; you are familiar with all my ways . . . Where can I go from your Spirit? Where can I flee from your presence? If I go up to the heavens, you are there; if I make my bed in the depths, you are there. If I rise

on the wings of the dawn, if I settle on the far side of the sea, even there your hand will guide me, your right hand will hold me fast.

—Psalm 139:1-3, 7-10 NIV

But though I was familiar with that biblical passage, I'd never gotten to know God intimately or fully embraced His love for me. Ever since my earliest childhood, I'd felt that my parents only expressed approval or positive interest when I did something good. Yes, I was aware that this was part of the culture in which they were raised, and I knew their critical comments and tone were done with good intentions to help me strive to be better. But though their negative comments did help me strive to improve myself, these comments also fostered deep resentments in me. Moreover, their critical expression was also directed toward each other and my siblings, which didn't help either.

I learned from this that a critical tongue deeply affects the spirit and self-esteem of those being criticized. But even though that trait affected me deeply, it was also how I in turn learned to behave toward others for many years. Over time, God opened my eyes about how hurtful my critical speech could be toward others, especially the people closest to me. God led me to the following verses especially in helping me address my own critical tongue.

As God's chosen ones, holy and beloved, clothe yourselves with compassion, kindness, humility, and patience. Bear with one another and, if anyone has a complaint against another, forgive each other; just as the Lord has forgiven you, so you also must forgive. Above all, clothe yourselves with love, which binds everything together in perfect harmony.

—Colossians 3:12-14, NRSV

Do not let any unwholesome talk come out of your mouths, but only what helps build others up according to their needs, that it may benefit those who listen.

—Ephesians 4:29 NIV

Therefore encourage one another and build each other up, just as you are doing.

—1 Thessalonians 5:11 NIV

My critical tongue and negativity affected many individuals as my parents' criticism had affected me and their parents' harsh words had undoubtedly affected them. God knows that we each need words of affirmation, and He wants His children to be different rather than continuing the generational cycle of criticism and blame. We need to love each other above all, and we need love with healthy boundaries and which uses constructive word choices.

SEVEN

信望愛

DOES GOD CARE?

B esides constantly feeling a need to seek approval, I lacked trust in God. This was because I didn't understand God's character. I saw God as being like my earthly dad, who didn't seem interested in me, my daily activities, or issues that bothered me. Since my earliest childhood, Dad was so involved in his non-profit, devoting all spare time outside of work to running it, that I could never depend on him being there for me.

God blessed me with my grandfather to fill that gap while we still lived in Taiwan. But moving to the United States brought to the surface my lack of trust in a God who seemed distant, absent, and too busy to care about my daily life issues.

Since I didn't feel I could rely on God or my parents to care about me, I compensated by endeavoring to maintain complete control over my life. My parents had taught me to be self-sufficient and not reliant on others. So I would make my plans with numerous backup plans to ensure that everything in my life was predictable.

Mom always emphasized getting a good education and having a career. She'd had a hard life and worked very hard to earn the needed income for our family so Dad could focus on his non-profit work. Despite having only a junior high education, she'd set herself to learn the necessary skills to become a small business owner in Taiwan before coming to the United States. Through this, she'd supported not only my dad and her children but other extended family like my paternal grandparents.

Because Mom had to help provide for so many family and relatives, she had very little for herself. It was with the best intentions based on her own experiences that Mom pushed me to do well so I could have a better future and not have to depend on anyone else. My parents also went through a lot of difficult challenges as two blind individuals. They had to learn to be self-sufficient since there was no government help for the disabled or their children in Taiwan, a trait they passed on to me and my brothers.

In consequence, I simply didn't realize that God was interested in being part of all the small things happening in my life. For a long time, I believed that God doesn't care about us. I know now that this was a big lie that Satan wants us to believe. God's Word makes clear that God not only cares about us but is always attentive to every aspect of our lives.

Give all your worries and cares to God, for he cares about you.

—1 Peter 5:7, NLT

You know when I sit and when I rise; you perceive my thoughts from afar.

—Psalm 139:2 NIV

Are not two sparrows sold for a penny? Yet not one of them will fall to the ground outside your Father's care. And even the very hairs of your head are all numbered. So don't be afraid; you are worth more than many sparrows.

—Matthew 10:29-31 NIV

God not only cares for me but loved me unconditionally even when I was still a sinner rejecting Him. And though He did and still does allow challenges and trials in my life, He does so for my ultimate benefit and His ultimate purpose.

God demonstrates his love for us in this: While we were still sinners, Christ died for us.

—Roman 5:8 NIV

And we know that in all things God works for the good of those who love him, who have been called according to his purpose.

—Romans 8:28 NIV

But though I knew these teachings were in the Bible, at the time they didn't mean much more to me than wise sayings on a page. Several significant events had to take place before I could see God's hand in my life.

The first of these critical life moments was a switch in my career choice. A couple years into my electrical engineering program, I applied and accepted a co-op internship with IBM. During the internship, I worked as a programmer mostly in isolation and only occasionally met with a team. In the evening, I would spend time with other co-op students socializing, learning ballroom dancing, and trying various foods from different ethnic backgrounds.

I gradually realized that electrical engineering was not where my passion resided or what I wanted to do as my career. As I reflected on what would make me strive as a person, I recognized that it was the relational factor provided through team collaboration. I also wanted to invest my life into doing something that would make the world a better place for others. The for-profit environment didn't align with my values. I give thanks to my parents for their daily example of devoting themselves to work with others in bettering the lives of the blind and others around them.

After finishing my nine months internship, I returned to university determined to find my own career path. I had no idea where I'd end up, but this is where I really began turning to God. By this point, I'd gone through my second baptism at the Baptist church. I had a deep desire to seek God and asked Him to show me what He had planned for me. But I still wasn't sure if the God I understood Him to be cared enough about me to give me guidance.

My faith at this moment was very much a baby faith. Thankfully, I was surrounded by some good Christian friends who were praying for me. I had to learn the characteristics and character of my heavenly Father, which were very different from my earthly dad. I ended up taking a summer break from school to research various career choices. Among these were law, medicine, and accounting. I even worked a part-time job as a teacher's assistant to try out teaching.

One day I attended a meeting of the Society of Women Engineers. A female civil engineer speaker described her job as a bridge engineer and how she worked in conjunction with the Texas Department of Transportation. At that moment, something in me sensed that civil engineer was the career I needed to pursue. Looking back, I can see that the Holy Spirit was tugging at my heart.

I then had to meet with the dean of UT's electrical engineering program to discuss transferring to the civil engineering program. He was not happy with me. I was a high A student, and he reminded me forthrightly that getting accepted into UT's electrical engineering program was difficult and an honor. Many candidates who were unable to get into the program would love to be in my position. He felt that a transfer to civil engineering would be wasting my great opportunity.

But whether or not it made sense to others, I was convicted that this was what God was calling me to do. I thanked the dean for his willingness to meet with me and talk through my choice. He still wanted me to reconsider and made clear that anyone who exited the program would not be able to re-enter. I responded honestly that I was aware of the consequences and that this simply demonstrated how seriously I took my choice of transferring to civil engineering.

The moment I made this irrevocable statement aloud, I had peace that my career change was not a mistake but the path God had laid out for me to strive forward. God blessed me in that most of the courses I'd taken under the electrical engineering program were transferable to the civil engineering program since the first two years of both programs were mostly basic engineering courses.

Then in my junior year, I came across courses in the field of water resources. This fascinated me since I saw water as one of the essential precious resources needed for all human beings to survive and thrive. I focused my remaining years of study at UT specifically to becoming an engineer in the field of water resources. This was a great turning point in my life journey. For the first time, I was making a major life choice that wasn't just to please and get approval from my parents but to seek out the path of where God was asking me to go.

EIGHT

信望愛

DIFFICULT DETOURS

W hen I reached my last summer of civil engineer studies, I had another three months outstanding of co-op obligation to complete. These are optional team programs that allow engineering students to gain real-world experience in their fields along with additional credit hours. The UT co-op program called me about an opening for a summer internship with the Fort Worth Water Department, which was only an hour from where my family lived in Dallas. While I had no idea then, this summer co-op opportunity proved to be the beginning of a long term career at the Fort Worth Water Department.

Over time, I've come to learn that a plan is a good guide to have, but we must allow for changes and detours along the way. As a planning engineer, I recognize that creating a master plan is our best effort to prepare for what may happen in the future. But when we try to implement them, things don't necessarily go according to even the best-laid plans because life intervenes with unexpected challenges that divert our path or create a detour.

God used this lesson to help me become less rigid. I had to learn that God was preparing me to lean on Him moment by moment and that He doesn't provide the entire detailed plan for our lives upfront. If He did, it would be too overwhelming and might paralyze us from moving forward.

Have you ever faced that dilemma? Have you gotten to a place where you plan everything out and stick to your list to the point of inflexibility despite what happens? In the past, I would run myself to exhaustion until I completed everything on my list. I hadn't learned how to balance being self-sufficient and trusting in God.

Over my college years, God was in the process of refining me little by little as a river smooths and polishes the rough edges of small rocks. Though I'd gone through baptism by immersion at the Baptist church my freshman year, I still didn't know there was far more to the Christian way of life than just being baptized. I thought being a Christian meant being friendly to people and not saying bad words or doing bad things. I couldn't even conceive that a Christian life meant knowing God intimately.

Since I didn't know God intimately at that time, I also didn't know how to trust God or ask the Holy Spirit to guide me in my everyday decisions. In fact, I wouldn't have known which plans were from God even if I'd been listening to Him.

During this time period, God brought a serious test of faith into my life through the dear friend who'd asked to date me. This young man had been the first to show me that being involved in a church home should be a joyful feeling and not a burden. But what I didn't know was that he himself had never accepted Christ into his heart. His enthusiasm about church had given me the impression that he had. But as a baby Christian myself, I had no idea what the characteristics were of a mature Christian.

What I came to realize was that the young man enjoyed Christian friendship because his church friends were very nice people who displayed love toward each other. They had become his family away from family while he was at university. But he wasn't yet at a place where he was interested in accepting Jesus Christ as his personal Savior and Lord.

We did end up dating on and off for five years. This became a major struggle in my life as I myself came to know more of God's love and increasingly desired to follow God. The Holy Spirit repeatedly brought this relationship to my attention, and every spring, summer, and winter break, I would try to break up with him. I did this in part because I felt he might find someone else during the breaks. But as I learned more about God and the Bible, I was also bothered by the idea of being in an intimate relationship with a non-believer. I knew this wasn't in line with biblical teaching and I believed one should only enter into a dating relationship if there is potential to marry.

But each time we returned to college from break, we would get back together. Looking back, I can see I had a lot of insecurities rooted in not fully realizing that God truly loved me unconditionally. I felt badly that I was putting my boyfriend through this kind of emotional roller coaster. Many times, I made up justifications to God as to why I should continue this relationship. I would focus on my boyfriend's authentic, loving, warm, and respectful personality. His willingness to help others. His enthusiastic attitude toward involvement in church activities.

But even in those few moments when my boyfriend's attentions convinced me I deserved to be loved and when I focused on all his good characteristics, I continue to feel the Holy Spirit tugging at me and giving me no peace about being "yoked together with an unbeliever" (2 Corinthians 6:14). I knew the difference in our belief systems would affect a long-term relationship, any future marriage, as well as family life.

Throughout those five years of college, I asked God why He couldn't just make my boyfriend believe in Him. God revealed to me that He loves us so much He must allow us the free will and time to choose Him for ourselves. I protested that this was clearly the best time for boyfriend to become a Christian. I'm aware that I was being pretty arrogant and selfish. I was essentially saying to God that I knew better than God Himself!

After five years of dating, this young man completed a master's degree since he'd begun advanced studies before I had. I graduated with a bachelor's degree in civil engineering. By then I'd grudgingly come to accept that God's timing is perfect even if I didn't like it, and we did break up permanently.

Just a few months later, my friend did accept Christ as his Savior. He also found another lovely Christian young woman to date, whom he eventually married. Though I rejoiced that he'd become a Christian, the timing of it and his new relationship hurt me deeply, building further resentment in me toward God. I would beg God to please open my eyes and help me see why He'd allowed this to happen. It took the next five years to heal my heart and teach me to be closer to God.

I also had to work on my perception of myself and embrace how God loves me. I wanted to be loved but didn't know how to receive love or give love. Maybe you've pushed someone away because you didn't believe you deserved their love. That was me. Along with lacking understanding of God's character, I didn't recognize the truth of my own identity in God's love. Though I was and am God's precious daughter, I continued believing all of Satan's lies. I was not in any physical bondage and was privileged to live in a free country. But I was allowing myself to remain in spiritual bondage, as the apostle Paul warns against.

> So Christ has truly set us free. Now make sure that you stay free and don't get tied up again in slavery to the law.
>
> —Galatians 5:1, NLT

Is something keeping you in slavery and chained to the past? If so, what is it that is stopping you from entering into God's freedom and promises?

NINE

信望愛

BUT GOD!

Still, God was slowly working in me. Still, God was slowly working in me. After college, God intervened in my life to bring me back to the Dallas/Fort Worth (DFW) area where I'd lived with my parents and had no desire to return. After graduation, I took a job as a graduate engineer in Austin. Six months into this job, my mom called, asking me to move back to the Dallas-Fort Worth (DFW) area where I could live at home and help her out more.

By this time, my youngest brother George was a freshman in the University of Texas aerospace program. My brother Jeff had ended up marrying a year after graduating from high school. He and his wife Jackie already had one daughter. While they lived near my mom, Jeff had a truck driving job that took him away from home a lot, and my sister-in-law was taking classes along with raising two children.

I can admit I was very selfish at this time, and moving back home was the last thing on my agenda. I wanted to stay in Austin with my friends. If I moved home, I had no doubt the freedom I'd been experiencing as a young adult would be hampered and I'd be stuck driving Mom everywhere again.

Another reason I didn't want to return home was because I didn't want to face the resentment I felt toward my mom. A couple events had contributed toward this. During my early teens, a friend of my dad's began tutoring my brothers and me in our schoolwork. He grew fond of me and proposed marriage several times before I was out of high school. I told him I didn't want to get married yet but had plans to go to college. He told me he'd be patient and wait.

Then during a visit home my freshman year of college, I told him of the young man I'd met and had started dating. He became so angry he tried to force himself on me. He was very strong with a black belt in martial arts, so I was terrified. But the Holy Spirit gave me a supernatural peace that allowed me to speak calmly to him, reminding him that this wasn't who he was and that I understood his hurt over my new relationship.

He eventually let me go. But when I told Mom what had happened, she replied that he was a very nice person and would never do such a thing. I was heartbroken that my own mother didn't trust me enough to believe what I'd told her.

Then during my sophomore year, an additional rift arose between my mom and me. My dad had asked me to get in contact with a pastor friend he had in Austin since my own parents weren't nearby if I ever had a need. I obediently visited the friend. His family wasn't home, and to my horror the pastor sexually propositioned me. I was shocked that a pastor responsible to God could behave in such a way, though I recognize now that even clergy are still sinners by nature. Thankfully, his family walked in just then, so I was able to get away.

I drove home to DFW to visit my mom, hoping she would comfort me. But when I told her of my experience, she immediately responded that the man was a pastor and would never do that, so whatever happened must have been my fault. That my own mom would think this of me hurt deeply and created even more resentment in me toward my mom.

Along with this resentment, I didn't want to be around her critical tongue and constantly worried, negative attitude. I told her I'd come back if someone offered me a job, comfortable in the knowledge that I hadn't applied to any graduate engineer position in any civil engineering company in the DFW area so I didn't have to worry about a job offer.

But God had very different plans. I'd spent the summer before my senior year of college doing a three-month co-op internship at the Fort Worth Water Department. When I'd finished, I'd informed my boss I wasn't interested in coming back to that area after graduation as I wanted to stay in Austin to be around my friends. But God has His ways. Somehow the very day after my mom called, my former boss in Fort Worth got my number, called me, and offered me a job on the spot.

"Is this for real?" I asked God.

I continued to resist. Since I'm pretty hardheaded, I figured that before yielding to God I'd ask for the kind of confirmation Gideon requested in the Old Testament story of laying out a fleece to test God's will (Judges 6:36-40). So I named a salary amount I was sure this company wouldn't be willing to grant. To my shock, my former boss got an HR (human resources) waiver for the salary amount, then called back to tell me they could match the salary I'd requested.

And here I'd been thinking I could outsmart God! That is the biggest joke, as Scripture reminds us.

We can make our plans, but the LORD determines our steps.

—Proverbs 16:9, NLT

And that was how I ended up back in DFW completely against my own wishes or plans. Have you ever had God spell something out so obviously it is impossible to miss? That was the case here. I could no longer doubt that God was telling me to move back to DFW. So after some extensive talking to God, I yielded to God's plan and took the job offer. I found a small apartment close enough to my mom that I could help her while giving both of us some independence.

But though God was showing me He did care and wanted to be involved in my daily life, even this very clear divine intervention didn't bring me completely around. Instead, I saw God as taking away both my freedom and my Austin friends. Also, I hated driving and having to drive my mom all over such a huge, congested city as well as the commute back and forth between Dallas where Mom lived and my job in Fort Worth left me a nervous wreck. Since this included weekends, as I'd feared I had little time for social activities or making new friends.

I began resenting God and wanted God to stay out of my life. I didn't understand that life's trials were the ways God would use to mature me and mold me so I could become what He planned for me to be. Nor did God want to leave me in this state of resentment against my mom. He wanted me to go home and heal that relationship, which in the end did come about as I will share later. This included learning to accept my parents for who they were instead of trying to make them meet my expectations of what a parent should be.

What I've come to realize is that God was taking me through a transformation process, one I was constantly resisting. The process is similar to a caterpillar changing into a butterfly that will one day take flight. The caterpillar has to change from the physical state of crawling on the ground with all its little legs to flying in the air with wings. These changes occur while it is hanging all wrapped up in a cocoon. During this time period, the caterpillar has to forego its previous mindset of moving along the ground for a completely new mindset of maneuvering through all the different aerodynamics necessary in using its new wings to fly.

This is a remarkable transformation. The Bible tells us that we will be similarly transformed as we allow our minds to renewed to follow God's pattern and perfect will rather than following the pattern of this world.

> Do not conform to the pattern of this world, but be transformed by the renewing of your mind. Then you will be able to test and approve what God's will is—his good, pleasing and perfect will.
>
> —Romans 12:2 NIV

After moving back in with my mom, I also began attending the non-denominational Asian church she attended and which I'd attended with my family in high school. I quickly went from regular attendance to becoming very involved in that church.

One thing I'd wondered about was whether my prior baptism when I was an elementary school student counted. Since that had been in a Presbyterian church, I'd been sprinkled rather than baptized by full immersion in water as the church I now attended taught and practiced. Also, the decision to be baptized was made by my parents for the entire family rather than as a personal proclamation of faith.

So I made the decision to be baptized by immersion at the Baptist church in Austin that I had attended with my college friends. On the day of my baptism, many of my church friends were there to encourage me and others being baptized. It was an amazing day as I felt the personal embrace of God's love and of being accepted by God and these people into God's church family. This act was just one step in my reaching out to God, who had been patiently waiting for me.

But though I'd gone through baptism by immersion and was active in church, I was still living a performance-based walk with God while seeking acceptance from others. Even being baptized by immersion had been an extra "just to make sure" assurance that God would accept me. My need for acceptance and approval from other Christians was fear-based instead of love-based, and I was still trying to live the Christian life my way, not God's way. My chosen path was directed by logic-driven decisions instead of Holy Spirit-driven decisions or a daily depend-ence on God.

This included exhausting my body with lots of planned activities. I helped in the church with the youth and college group as well as other areas where volunteers were needed. I worked forty hours a week at the Fort Worth Water Department. I spent many hours commuting between where my mom lived in Dallas to Fort Worth and driving her around. I also devoted at least twenty hours a week practicing ballroom dancing since it was my ambition to compete in that art form.

All of this was work-based instead of love-based, and I got very little sleep, which left me increasingly exhausted and sleep-deprived. Once in a while for some major decision, I would ask God for direction, but I didn't know to seek guidance through the Holy Spirit for daily deci-sions, whether big or small. Nor did I seek God's guidance when a need arose as to whether that need was for me to fulfill or someone else. By automatically taking those needs on myself, I was taking someone else's opportunity to serve God and ended up spending my time in areas God never intended.

I also continued to see God as a remote authority up in heaven rather than a loving heavenly Father who wanted to love and embrace me. In truth, I didn't understand the real meaning of either grace or love. I didn't want to surrender control of my life to God because I still lacked trust in His loving care for me. I kept relying on my self-sufficiency, operating out of what was logical to the human mind instead of seeking God's heart and plan for me.

Since I didn't have a good relationship with my heavenly Father or truly trust Him to have my best interests in mind, I found it easier to believe that my own path was the best. After all, no one else knew me better than myself—or so I thought. To place my complete trust in a God I didn't really know was to risk getting hurt.

I came to realize over time how wrong and spiritually blind I was. My parents were phys-ically blind, yet they seemed far more at ease with their trust in God than I did as a physically sighted but a spiritually blind person. We often can't see God's perspective due to the filters over our vision created by our past experiences and our emotional baggage from those experiences. God reminds us through His words to the prophet Isaiah:

Forget the former things; do not dwell on the past.

—Isaiah 43:18 NIV

What this reminder is telling us is not to allow our past experiences to tint our perception of the present and the future. This tinting can keep us in a holding pattern because we are giving our circumstances greater power than our amazing God.

God has a plan for us. He is just waiting for us to be willing. Our willingness has to come from yielding our own plans and actions to trust instead in how God operates.

God can use all our circumstances for our benefit to carry out His plan for us (Romans 8:28), even negative circumstances that come about because we deviate from His plan. This spiritual insight given by the Holy Spirit gave me a glimpse of how awesome our God is.

In the end, my body protested at all the over-activity. I had also become very thin as I wasn't eating healthily and at 5'5" had dropped in weight to under a hundred pounds. After a number of medical tests, the doctors diagnosed me with chronic fatigue. They had no solution as to when or if my body would recover except total rest. I had to take a medical leave from my job and ended up moving back home with my mom for several months, where I found myself sleep-ing up to eighteen hours a day.

During this physical time out, I spent a lot of time praying and talking to God. My mom also had to take care of me instead of our usual pattern of me caring for her. She dosed me with lots of Asian herbal medicine and chicken soup. I began to regain some of my lost weight and strength. More importantly, during this time together with Mom caring for me, we were finally able to have some crucial heart-to-heart talks, which went a long way to heal our relationship.

Ten

信望愛

Marriage and Heartbreak

After three months of complete rest, my body recovered, and I was able to return back to work. My doctors did emphasize that I needed to minimize my travel and activities. Taking their advice, I moved away from my mom's home to Fort Worth, which greatly reduced my travel hours. Once settled into my new living arrangement, I started looking for a home church and a place to continue my ballroom dancing.

I ended up meeting my future husband at a ballroom dancing class I signed up for at Fort Worth's recreational center. Of Caribbean heritage, he was more than a decade older than me, divorced with no kids, and came from a strong Christian background. Raised in the Assembly of God denomination, he'd gone on many missionary trips and had gotten a bachelor's degree at an Assembly of God college. But over the years, he'd been sidetracked from his Christian faith.

Though there'd been a lot of healing in my relationship with my mom, I was still not very mature as a Christian or strong in my faith walk with God, and I really needed to focus on developing my personal relationship with God and restoring the broken relationship with my dad. But I very quickly got sidetracked and ended up focusing instead on developing a relationship with my future husband. We talked to each other every day. He didn't have a home church, and I was also looking for one in Fort Worth. So together we found a Baptist church to attend and both got involved in ministry there. I also wanted to enroll in the family counseling program at Fort Worth's Southwestern Baptist seminary, and he gave me pointers on how to apply.

After just one month of dating, I invited my Dallas friends to Fort Worth to meet my new boyfriend. I have very protective friends, and they grilled him for a long time before giving their approval. We continued dating, and all was going well. We were serving God together at our church. We were also both at a very good place in our careers. He'd just found a new job, and I had a stable job at the Fort Worth Water Department. He'd met my family and many of my Dallas friends. I'd met his friends but not his family since they lived in Toronto, Canada.

But after six months of dating, he hadn't shown any interest in moving on to the next phase of our relationship, and I began struggling as to whether we should continue this relationship. We'd been very respectful of each other, and since I knew he'd been married and divorced before, I didn't want to continue on if he needed more time to heal and wasn't ready for a new relationship.

On New Year's Day 1999 when I was together with him, I asked God to bring the right words to my mouth to talk about our next step. But just as I opened my mouth, he began speaking. At that moment, the Holy Spirit quieted my thoughts and instructed that I let my boyfriend speak first. He proceeded to propose marriage to me, and I said yes.

We traveled to Toronto to visit his family. They were so warm and loving. His mom is a very devoted Christian as are some of his other family members. The extended family living in Toronto is quite large, and they threw a welcoming party where I met his sister, brother, sister-in-law, uncles, aunts, cousins, nieces, and nephews, in all at least forty-plus people who were all close relatives. Having such a small family myself in North America, I was surprised.

We were married in 2000. My brother George was married that same year to a lovely Christian young woman he'd met at his church. Dad made an extensive visit from Taiwan during this time period, taking a temporary massage job at the Fort Worth

YMCA. So he was able to be at both weddings. Dad and I had hardly spoken in years except for short phone calls, so our reunion felt awkward. But we did have a nice conversation before my wedding. Dad asked if I was sure this was what I wanted and if my husband-to-be was good to me. I described how attentive and considerate he was.

After the wedding, we both focused on work and building a house in Saginaw, TX area. We also continued to be involved in the church where we'd been serving together, but my dependence on God was not very strong. I was depending more on my spouse at that time. Many times, I allowed my self-sufficiency and pride to get in the way, traits that continued throughout my marriage, derailing me from following God's plan for my life.

On top of that, I had never addressed the deep anger and resentment I'd allowed to build up over the years. These emotions were pent up inside of me like a sleeping, angry lion. When I met my husband, he gave me attention and cherished me. We were very focused on each other, and for a while I was very happy.

But our very busy schedules and long work hours began pushing us apart. He'd gone through a difficult first marriage and was dealing with his own pain. I was aware I could be grumpy and irritable after a tiring day of work. Both of us were somewhat older when we married—I was thirty years old and he forty-one—and set in our own ways to the point of unyielding stubbornness.

We'd been married about three years when I became pregnant with my oldest daughter. The pregnancy was a smooth one with no complications, and our oldest daughter joined us in 2004. I don't recall having any real conflicts or arguments during our marriage before her birth. But not long after she was born, we both began expressing very different ideas of how to raise her, and neither of us were willing to back down.

Disagreement seeped deeper and deeper into our marriage. During these conflicts, my pent-up anger would surface. Occasionally, we let God in and put our own ideas aside to compromise. But once again, I wasn't seeking the Holy Spirit's guidance daily. We would follow our own logic of what needed done instead of asking God to show us what was best for the family as whole. While God was there, He was definitely not first in our lives.

It didn't help that oldest daughter was a high-need baby. She suffered greatly from colic and allergies for her first eighteen months especially. We were not getting much sleep, and since my husband and I both worked, stress from our jobs and busy schedule compounded our exhaustion. When stress increased, the sleeping angry lion in me would wake up with a big roar, and I found myself defaulting to how I'd seen my parents deal with life stress and marital conflicts.

By this time, I was not seeking God very often. Have you ever let God into your life only occasionally or just kept God completely at bay? You may think you are still in control, but believe me you are not! It wasn't easy attending church with a constantly crying baby, so we gradually phased out of attendance or involvement in our church.

Meanwhile, the frequency of those lion roars increased as time went on. Have you ever TOLD OTHERS THAT YOU DO NOT HAVE AN ANGER PROBLEM WHILE SHOUTING IN ALL CAPS AT THEM!!!???? Several friends tried to talk to me about my anger, but I dismissed them. I was in denial that I had an anger problem. I had no idea how giant the iceberg was under the surface of the water.

My husband and I did our best to continue on, focusing mainly on our oldest daughter instead of our relationship with each other or with God. By now, my mom had moved back to Taiwan to be with my dad. Every two years or so, she'd travel to the United States to visit her children. My dad never came with her. But in 2005, my brothers and I and our spouses and children all traveled to Taiwan to celebrate my paternal grandmother's ninetieth birthday and to visit my maternal grandmother, who was in hospice in a Tainan hospital and passed away shortly after our visit. This was my brothers' first trip back to Taiwan since we'd left.

Then I went back to school for fifteen months to obtain my executive MBA. My husband had always supported my right to pursue a career as much as his own and encouraged me to continue my education. But the added busyness and stress of completing a master's program just compounded the strain on our marriage. By the time I'd completed my master's degree program, we were really struggling in our relationship. Still, we pressed on for several years, doing our best to focus on our careers and our oldest daughter.

Then in 2009 when our oldest daughter was five years old, we discussed having a second child. I had my concerns about another child, since I felt this would put even more strain on our marriage if we didn't first address the problems in our relationship. Also, though both of us were working long hours, we had no household help. My husband didn't want strangers in his house. This was already becoming unsustainable. How could we even handle more responsibilities if we didn't get some additional help?

I prayed about having another child, and while I was still not sure, God gave me the comfort that it would be okay to move forward. I did get pregnant, and our second daughter was born the summer of 2010. Despite some high risk factors due to my age, her pregnancy was also a smooth one. We'd braced ourselves for a similar experience as we'd had with our oldest daughter, but God had a different plan. Our second daughter was soon sleeping through the night without any issues. Full of laughter and smiles, she brought joy to our family during a time when we faced our biggest relationship challenge yet.

Despite an adorable new daughter, our marriage was not in a good place, and I myself was in bad shape spiritually and emotionally. Like me, my husband was struggling with pent-up anger from events of his past, and though he'd pushed for another child, having a new baby in his early fifties was simply more than he'd anticipated. This created a lot of conflict with plenty of fault on both sides. Both of us found ourselves reverting to patterns we'd learned from our own parents with lots of raised voices and harsh words.

Still, I remained deeply in denial as to how far apart we'd drifted. My second daughter was only around three months old when my husband informed me he wanted to separate and planned to file for divorce. I couldn't believe my ears. How had he gone from wanting me to bear another child for us to raise together to asking for a separation and potential divorce?

I was stunned and heartbroken. I couldn't imagine how I was to take care of two small girls on my own while holding down a full-time job. My heart was in so much pain, but when I was in greatest despair, my second daughter would lift my spirits with one of her amazing smiles. She was such a Godsend to me as well as to her big sister and my husband as well. God also blessed me with a boss who understood the pain of divorce as he'd been through it himself many years earlier.

PICTURES

Dad's mentor Dr. Chen Wu Fu and his classmates. Dad is in
the second row fourth from the right with sunglasses on.

Dad taking notes using a braille typewriter while listening to a reel-to-reel audio tape recorder.

Dad in cap and gown for graduation
from Taiwan Theology Seminary.

Dad in his early twenties.

Mom in her early twenties.

Dad and Mom when
they were dating.

Dad and Mom's wedding picture in 1969.

Below: A field trip for the Taipei Benevolent Educational Society for the Blind led by Dad and Mom, my brother Jeff and me in the front row.

Above: A-Gong, Dad, Mom, my uncle, my brother Jeff, and me at the same field trip.

A-Gong standing in front of bookshelves he made for the Taipei Talking Books Library for the Blind.

With my mom and brothers Jeff and George during first trip to the United States in 1979.

Speaking as president of Key Club during my senior year in high school.

My freshman year of college in 1991.

Dad and Mom visiting Mr. John T. Brown, who helped us come to the United States, to thank him.

Dad and Mom at a Bible study/prayer meeting held at the Taipei Talking Books Library for the Blind.

My maternal grandmother visiting us in the United States in 1993. Left to right: my youngest brother George, me, Dad, Grandmother, Mom, my brother Jeff's wife, their oldest daughter, and Jeff.

My youngest brother George and me at Enchanted Rock, Texas in 1995.

Mom and me visiting friends from my college engineering co-op program in Los Angeles, 1995.

Dad and Mom at George's University at Texas graduation in 1998.

Below: Celebrating my paternal grandmother's ninetieth birthday on a trip to Taiwan with George (left back), his wife, Jeff's wife, Jeff, me, my husband at the time, oldest daughter, Dad (front left), paternal grandmother, and Mom.

Mom's family at my maternal grandmother's funeral. *Front row:* Mom's two sisters and brother and their spouses with Mom in the middle. *Back row:* Me, my oldest daughter, brother George, and cousins.

My two daughters and me in 2011.

God Can Take the Broken Pieces of Our Lives and Create a Beautiful

Person... Just Like We Can Take Little Pieces Make a Stained Glass Window!

Stained-glass art made by my sweet oldest daughter during a divorce care class for kids.

信望愛

Faith, Hope, and Love.

Eleven

信望愛

When God Says Enough is Enough!

I mentioned at the beginning of this story how I'd allowed fears and obstacles to dominate my mind so that my life seemed one huge, impassable mountain range I came to see as my personal Mount Himalaya. Did you know that the Himalayan mountain range has over a hundred major mountain peaks that stretch for more than twenty-five hundred kilometers? Ten of the planet's tallest fourteen peaks are located in the Himalayas and more than fifty peaks that measure above seven thousand meters in height.

Maybe you feel as though you feel as though life has placed peak after peak of trials in front of you to climb. I know I felt like I'd climbed any number of high, difficult peaks by this point in my own life. There were several significant Mt. Himalaya experiences I'd gone through that I haven't yet mentioned.

One such Himalayan peak occurred not long after I'd moved back to DFW to work for the Fort Worth Water Department. I was a passenger in a car driven by a co-worker when the vehicle was involved in a major car accident. We were stopped at a red light. A driver coming up behind us was on her cell phone and didn't notice that the light had turned red. She rear-ended us at full speed, totaling our vehicle. The accident left me with spine injuries that resulted in temporarily paralyzing one side of my body. I eventually had to undergo neck surgery to permanently alleviate the spinal nerve damage.

Another peak was getting mugged twice within a month a couple years into my move back to DFW. The worse incident occurred when I'd headed out to meet some church friends for a bite after a late fellowship get-together. I'd parked outside the restaurant where my friends were waiting for me. I was getting out of my car when another car pulled up in the parking lot beside me. Someone in the passenger's seat opened their door and tried to grab my purse off my shoulder.

I immediately pushed my door against their door to keep the person from getting out while also trying to pull my purse away. That was when they sprayed me in the face with pepper spray. I screamed, pushing my door even harder against their door. Thankfully, my friends heard me and came rushing out. The thief released my purse, and their car sped away. But the pain of the pepper spray in my eyes was as though my eyes were being eaten alive. It felt like I was going blind just as had happened to my parents.

Not even the paramedics when they showed could do anything to ease my pain. They told me I just needed to cry it out until my tears washed away the spray. I am so deeply thankful God permitted me to be surrounded by my church friends when this happened. Despite the enormous pain, I felt their care and love and experienced God's presence and assurance that I would be okay.

The second mugging also happened as I was leaving a restaurant with friends after a meal. We were all walking spread out in a sizeable group toward our cars. I was in the middle of our pack with another friend. Suddenly, a small guy with a hat came running through our group and grabbed at my purse strap. I refused to release my purse. As we fought, the thief and I both landed on top of a nearby car hood. My friends responded to my screams and ran toward me. At that, the thief chose to let go and ran away.

Both events were extremely traumatic and terrifying. But each time, God protected me and prevented the loss of my belongings, one more example of my heavenly Father's care and protection even at a time when I was living with an angry, resentful attitude toward God.

Beyond these incidents, another major mountain peak was an ongoing heart condition called tachycardia, where my heart would race from two hundred to three hundred beats per minute without any prior notice. This caused my heart to run out of blood to pump, at which point I would pass out. For most of my life, I wasn't aware of why this was happening, and my previous doctors had never spotted the condition.

Then in 2006 when my oldest daughter was a toddler, I experienced the worst such episode yet. My husband was just leaving for work, and I was closing the garage door behind him. Before the garage door fully closed, I passed out and hit the garage floor. Thankfully, my husband saw me and rushed back in to help. In short, God's plan for my life here on this earth was not yet finished, and He placed my husband in just the right spot at just the right moment to be able to get help for me.

I ended up undergoing atrioventricular node ablation, a surgical procedure that destroys the electrical signaling connection causing the issue. During the surgery, I had another episode of tachycardia. The surgeon later told me that they rarely observe the heart experiencing tachycardia while doing the procedure, so most patients with this condition end up with a pacemaker. Because I had an episode while in surgery, the doctors were able to identify the exact spot in my heart to treat. In consequence, I didn't need a pacemaker or ongoing medication.

Once again, God was showing me that even during these difficult Mt. Himalaya moments, He was there with me. When the peaks seemed too difficult for me to climb on my own, He sent others to help me through the trials.

By far the most difficult mountain peak I faced, far higher than those that had come before, the Mt. Everest of my personal Himalayan mountain range, was the breakup of my marriage. When I'd heard previously of someone getting a divorce, I'd never recognized how much hurt and pain they were going through. Divorce is heart-wrenching with many lives destroyed and many dreams lost.

But this also became the most significant turning point of my life that God used to propel me toward spiritual freedom and intimacy with Him. It was during this time that I came to truly understand that God never abandons us. He will always there with us through our Himalayan mountain peaks of life trials if we are willing to acknowledge Him.

When I went through the breakup of my marriage, I was still on maternity leave with my newborn second daughter as well as caring for my sweet seven-year-old firstborn. Nursing my second daughter and caring for my seven-year-old took all my energy during this period of emotional trauma. During the day,

I put on a smile as much as I could for the girls. Just getting through each hour minute by minute was a struggle. The emotional hurts were deep and took so much out of me that I even had to put instructions on the microwave to remember how to use it. I would focus on getting the kids fed, cleaned, and off to bed. Then I would cry until no tears were left.

My parents were both back in Taiwan while my brother George and his family now lived in Houston. My brother Jeff and his family were in the DFW area, but Jeff worked long hours, and his wife was very busy with her own growing family. So I had no family close by to help me. Nor did they know how to give advice in this situation. They tried to comfort me, but they didn't know what to do.

My friends also tried to comfort me, but most had never been through a divorce so they couldn't really empathize. They did try to help by talking to my ex-husband. But he was not interested in going to counseling or working toward the restoration of our marriage.

Of course, it takes both sides to have the will to reverse challenges in a marriage. Back then, I was very structured and black/white in my thoughts while he was not. I wanted to take charge to force a reconciliation, but he was done with our marriage and just wanted to move on. Also, he was not open in talking about deep emotional struggles and issues, so it was hard to know what he was feeling and thinking. It soon became clear that he'd moved on to a new relationship.

In all of this, I wasn't leaning on God or trusting that God was working for my ultimate good despite the situation. I wasn't part of any church family at this time, so I had no spiritual support from other Christians either. I didn't have the energy to talk to others or visit with anyone, so I ended up isolating myself from the outside world. I was too stubborn and hurt to recognize that God was there with me the whole time, and my pain was too loud for me to hear God's Holy Spirit speaking to me.

But it was also during this same heart-wrenching time period that I began crying out to God, and God in turn was able to use my brokenness to reach in and begin breaking down the tall, thick walls I'd built to keep Him and others out. God also gave me perspective in my brokenness through the following promises.

> The Lord is close to the brokenhearted and saves those who are crushed in spirit.
>
> —Psalm 34:18 NIV

> He [God] will give a crown of beauty for ashes, a joyous blessing instead of mourning, festive praise instead of despair. In their righteousness, they will be like great oaks that the LORD has planted for his glory.
>
> —Isaiah 61:3, NLT

But it wasn't just emotional pain and grief I was struggling with. I was also dealing with overwhelming fear. My maternity leave would soon be over, and I had no idea how I was going to juggle returning to work with caring for a newborn and seven year old on my own. The thought of raising two small daughters as a single parent with only a minimal support system while also working to pay off a large debt my husband and I had built up during our marriage was terrifying.

One day during those early months of our marriage separation, I was driving on the highway, heading out to run an errand, when my fears and questions engulfed me. How was I going to survive financially? How could I care adequately for my two precious daughters and also work? What if I failed to be the loving mother to them I'd always longed to be? If I hadn't been able to make it work with two parents in the home, how could I make it work as a single mom?

The devastating wave of fear and worry sweeping over me nearly broke me. I started crying uncontrollably even as I drove down the highway, crushed under a weight of sadness and hopelessness. But just at that moment as I looked down the road, I saw a billboard that belonged to Grace Baptist Church, a large church located northwest of Fort Worth. In huge font, it read:

"Do Not Fear for I Am with You." —God

WOW! I thought as I drove past. *That is really comforting!*

Then it occurred to me that most church billboards usually show service times and that week's sermon topic. When I drove back past the billboard on my way home from my errand, I saw that the billboard now only displayed the service times.

That's when I realized our gracious heavenly Father had divinely used the church billboard to send me a personal message of comfort, reassuring me that I didn't need to be afraid because God was, is, and will always be with me. He even used the church's name "Grace" to show me that He is full of grace and here with me.

God has taught me that fear is not from Him as the apostle Paul reminded his protégé and disciple Timothy when that young missionary was dealing with a difficult ministry, health problems, and people problems.

> For God gave us a spirit not of fear but of power and love and self-control.
>
> —2 Timothy 1:7, ESV

Over and over in Scripture, God tells us not to be afraid because He is always with us and will be the one to uphold us and help us.

Don't be afraid, for I am with you. Don't be discouraged, for I am your God. I will strengthen you and help you. I will hold you up with my victorious right hand.

—Isaiah 41:10, NLT

Have I not commanded you? Be strong and courageous. Do not be afraid; do not be discouraged, for the Lord your God will be with you wherever you go.

—Joshua 1:9 NIV

(see also Genesis 26:24; Deuteronomy 31:6; 2 Kings 6:16; Isaiah 35:4; 43:1-2; Jeremiah 46:27-28; Acts 18:9-10).

Throughout this difficult season of my life, God continued to remind me not to be afraid, that He was always with me, and that He would be my provider. And He continues to remind me of this vital truth today. I've also learned that God can speak through all communication channels. My heavenly Father has spoken to me through Christian radio stations, devotionals, gospel music, church sermons, church signs, movies I've watched, even my baby's mouth. His continuous repeated message to me as His precious, beloved daughter includes:

I love you,

I respect you,

I cherish you,

I embrace you,

I encourage you.

I am your rock,

I am your strength,

I am your provider,

I am your comforter.

I will not reject you,

I am not critical of you,

~and~

I will not ever abandon you.

TWELVE

信望愛

A LOVING
HEAVENLY FATHER

What was your experience with your earthly father? Did he treat you indifferently, or were you embraced with love? Was there little interaction, or did you have memorable quality time together? Were you cared for or criticized, ridiculed, verbally abused, or even physically abused? Did you have loving thoughts toward your earthly father or more unpleasant, negative feelings?

Some of us are unable to fathom our heavenly Father as loving. Just the thought of the father figure many have known would deter them from any belief that God is a "good, good Father" as the gospel chorus goes. Is this because we associate our heavenly Father with our earthly father's absence, abandonment, or abuse? These may be tough questions.

These experiences and deeply-rooted emotions toward our earthly fathers can become a barrier that prevents many people from risking getting to know their heavenly Father. The emotional baggage we carry from our earthly father gets carried over into our relationship with our heavenly Father, keeping us from a beautiful, loving, and close relationship with God that He intended for us.

Conversely, maybe you had the privilege of experiencing a relationship with a loving, kind, caring earthly father. If that is your experience, then how you perceive your heavenly Father may be very different. You may be able to understand and embrace our loving heavenly Father with no hesitation.

In coming to know and understand God as my heavenly Father, I had to overcome my feelings about my earthly dad, who didn't express his affection toward his family. He didn't know how to give hugs or say, "I love you." He was interested in our educational development but not emotionally available for his family.

Overcoming this emotional baggage was not an easy journey. The distance between me and my earthly father as well as my heavenly Father had left a vast chasm in my heart only God could fill. But it took a long time for me to figure this out. I would try to speak and act like I was strong and didn't need anyone else or all that warm and fuzzy feel-good stuff. But it was just a cover-up. I'd built up a wall so tall and thick no one could see I was hurting that badly.

Though inside I needed my God so desperately, I looked for other ways to fill that need. Busyness and the pursuit of my education, goals, and hobbies temporarily filled the big hole in my heart. My self-esteem was very low due to the misbelief that I wasn't worthy of being loved by either my earthly father or my heavenly Father. That was so wrong but exactly what Satan wanted me to believe.

Then came the deep pain of my broken marriage but also the sweetness as I cried out to God and God reached out to me in a growing intimacy I'd never experienced in all the decades of attending church and thinking of myself as a Christian. God spoke to me through one verse in particular.

Be still and know that I am God.

—Psalm 46:10 NIV

"Do you know what this means, Wendy?" God asked me. "To know ME personally, intimately? To truly understand who I am and that I am God?"

What did intimacy with God even mean? I began to ponder the question. If I knew another human being intimately, I would know what their true character was. I would also know what their true nature *wasn't*.

In 2011 some months into my marriage separation and after my return to work at the Fort Worth Water Department, I started visiting a Baptist church in North Richland Hills, TX, where I was invited to a Sunday School class on the attributes of God. I had plenty of head knowledge on this topic, but God wanted me to know Him in my heart and build a close intimate relationship with Him. To get to know and understand God intimately, I had to first learn and understand who He was, including His different character traits.

God knew exactly what I needed, and through that Sunday school class He provided the way for me to get to know him. What I discovered from that study was that my heavenly Father didn't display my earthly father's characteristics or behaviors at all. I'd known this already in my head, but this time it was imprinted into my heart. God is love, grace, patience, forgiveness, holiness, lovingkindness, sovereign, almighty, just, merciful, omnipresent, and faithful to name just a few of His unique characteristics. God's Word in the following scriptures also reassured me.

> The Lord himself goes before you and will be with you; he will never leave you nor forsake you. Do not be afraid; do not be discouraged.
>
> —Deuteronomy 31:8 NIV

The Lord will fight for you; you need only to be still.

—Exodus 14:14 NIV

Why, even the hairs of your head are all numbered. Fear not; you are of more value than many sparrows.

—Luke 12:7, ESV

You formed the way I think and feel. You put me together in my mother's womb. I praise you because you made me in such a wonderful way. I know how amazing that was! You could see my bones grow as my body took shape, hidden in my mother's womb. You watched my body grow there. In your book, you wrote about all the days planned for me before any of them had happened.

—Psalm 139:13-16, ESV

As I learned to be intimate with God by fully experiencing Him in the daily events of my life, God showed me His grace, patience, forgiveness, mercy, and loving-kindness to build my faith and trust in Him. He has shown me daily in so many little ways how precious I am to Him and how much He loves me. Gradually, I came to understand that God created me uniquely and loves me just the way He made me. As I let my great wall slowly crumble down, I was able to experience God's amazing love daily.

And the more I was able to accept God's loving embrace, comfort, and healing, the more I was able to turn around and "pay forward" God's blessings to others as Scripture tells us we are to do with the love and comfort God gives us.

Praise be to the God and Father of our Lord Jesus Christ, the Father of compassion and the God of all comfort, who comforts us in all our troubles, so that we can comfort those in any trouble with the comfort we ourselves receive from God.

—2 Corinthians 1:3-4 NIV

And God is able to bless you abundantly, so that in all things at all times, having all that you need, you will abound in every good work.

—2 Corinthians 9:8 NIV

Thirteen

信望愛

Paying It Forward

I f the breakup of my marriage was my personal Mt. Everest, overcoming the pain of my divorce was my own personal ascent up the highest peak of my life trials, a climb that would have been impossible without God's help and strength. During this heartrending season yet intimately sweet time with my heavenly Father, it never occurred to me that my difficult life journey, emotional upheaval, messy relationships, and brokenness would have anything of value to offer others. So I was amazed when God began using the adversities of my difficult marriage separation and divorce to be my testimony to others.

My ex-husband and I went through a full year of mediation in trying to work out divorce terms and custody negotiations acceptable to us both. The divorce became final in 2013. One blessing was that my ex-husband not only contributed with child support but continued to be an involved, loving father and very protective of his daughters. I know many divorced fathers are not involved in their children's lives, so I appreciated that, and over time we developed a civil, respectful approach to co-parenting.

That said, the responsibilities of raising two small children as a single parent, especially when my youngest daughter was still an infant, were far from easy. My demanding job schedule made it a daily challenge to get from work to my girls' childcare center before they closed, then get home to cook a healthy meal for the girls, check on my oldest daughter's homework, put them to bed, and make the necessary preparations for the next day. My oldest daughter had to grow up a lot faster than her peers to help care for her younger sister while I dealt with other chores. She has always been a great big sister and such a blessing from God.

Not long into my marriage separation, I began attending divorce care classes at my new church home. Childcare was provided during the sessions, and for older children there was a divorce care class on their own level, which my older daughter attended. The Holy Spirit told me to continue with this class until I'd worked out my hurt, and my pain was so deep I ended up attending continuously for several years.

Since attendance varied a lot, we started each session sharing our basic backstory. In the beginning, I didn't see the point as I couldn't see how telling strangers my situation would help anyone else in this group. The story of how my undealt-with anger and resentment had hurt the marriage. Being a single mom to a young infant and an older child while working fulltime and no other family member's help. My ex-husband's unwillingness to do marriage counseling and the feelings of betrayal when he moved on to a new relationship. I was hurting so much I didn't even have the energy to help myself, much less share such personal details with others.

Also, though I was back at work with a steady income and receiving some child support, I felt the constant pressure of heavy debt that had built up during our marriage as well as other financial worries. All during my growing up years and young adulthood, I'd felt the burden of having blind parents depending on me and the responsibilities that entailed. Now I had two young daughters depending on me, and I was frantic not to let them down. I was letting the same anxiety and worries I'd criticized in my mom overwhelm me. I understood better how frightening it must have been to be the sole financial support for three children after my dad returned to Taiwan, not just as a single mom but a blind one with no family around to help.

But all my worries and concerns were not from God. The Holy Spirit gently told me that I only needed to tell my story, nothing more and nothing less. And sure enough, as I obeyed the Holy Spirit's prompting, sharing my story became the beginning of my healing and reconciliation with God.

Divorce care is a multi-week program. Usually participants attend just one series of sessions. In contrast, each time the program ended, I came back and attended it all over again. After a couple years of my participation, the program coordinator asked if I would take over as facilitator.

How can I facilitate when I'm still trying to figure things out myself? I remember thinking.

But the Holy Spirit again reminded me that I only needed to tell my story, nothing more and nothing less. Each time I told my story, God showed me how I was growing more intimately closer to Him and learning to lean more on Him. My tone and attitude also changed. The hurt and anger I'd brought to this sharing time turned into love, compassion, and empathy for others going through similar situations. Admittedly, I still had my moments, but God also taught me that He loved me no matter where I was in life.

Like the picture my sweet oldest daughter made during this time of heartbreak in her own divorce care class, God was working a beautiful masterpiece out of my brokenness as I learned to lean on Him and partner with Him. God was embracing me as a loving Father and assuring me that He was here with me, would comfort me, provide for my needs, and heal my heart. The pent-up resentment I'd felt toward God during so many years when I'd felt He didn't care about me melted into a heart overflowing with joy and praise and thanksgiving for my wonderful heavenly Father and all the blessings past, present and future He was pouring out on me.

Amidst the trials and struggles of divorce and single parenthood, I have come to understand that praising God and rejoicing in Him has helped me focus on who God truly is and maintain an attitude of gratitude for all He has done for me. Here are a few of my own favorite verses on praising and rejoicing in our heavenly Father.

> I will extol the Lord at all times; his praise will always be on my lips. I will glory in the Lord; let the afflicted hear and rejoice. Glorify the Lord with me; let us exalt his name together. I sought the Lord, and he answered me; he delivered me from all my fears.
>
> —Psalm 34:1-4 NIV

> I will exalt you, Lord, for you lifted me out of the depths and did not let my enemies gloat over me. Lord my God, I called to you for help, and you healed me. You, Lord, brought me up from the realm of the dead; you spared me from going down to the pit. Sing the praises of the Lord, you his faithful people; praise his holy name.
>
> —Psalm 30:1-4 NIV

> Always be joyful. Never stop praying. Be thankful in all circumstances, for this is God's will for you who belong to Christ Jesus.
>
> —1 Thessalonians 5:16-18 NIV

Focusing on God puts my challenging situation in perspective. My problems are not the big mountains I think they are but merely little pebbles in a small pond. You may have very different issues going on in your life than my own. But I hope and pray that you've come to trust with me that our heavenly Father is always a lot bigger than all of our concerns, worries, and challenges. God has already gone ahead of us to work out all the details, and God is just waiting for us to understand and thank Him for being God.

One of the ways God guided me to recognize the blessings in my life was through the well-known gospel hymn "Count your blessings." I encourage you to seek out and read the entire song, but here is just the first stanza.

COUNT YOUR BLESSINGS

When upon life's billows you are tempest-tossed,

When you are discouraged, thinking all is lost,

Count your many blessings, name them one by one,

And it will surprise you what the Lord has done.

The Holy Spirit whispered to me to focus on what I have, what I am grateful for, what my many blessings are, and not what I lack. I've tended to spend so much time inside my mind on what I've lacked that I ended up having an imbalance of thought life. It may be hard initially to count each thing we are grateful for. But as we slowly accumulate the many grateful blessings we can name, our perspective will start shifting.

During these challenging times, uncertainties and unknowns tend to lead our emotions, feelings, and thoughts down a path focused on our circumstances as though they are impossible to overcome. They tend to lead us to fear. When that happens, we resort back toward what is familiar like the Israelites wanting to go back to Egypt after being freed instead of heading joyously to the Promised Land (Numbers 13:1-14:4). When we let fear, anxiety, and worry dominate our thoughts, we miss God's blessings in our lives. How much God blesses us and loves us tends to be minimized or completely forgotten when we give our circumstances greater attention than they deserve.

In contrast, when I start listing all the many things big and small with which God has blessed me, including my current circumstances and my life journey to this point, God brings me from fear to gratefulness, thankful thoughts, and attitudes. We should consider counting our blessings and shifting our perspective toward gratitude for how God has carried us, whether through an emotional desert, over a small hill, or even up a huge spiritual Mount Everest.

Fourteen

信望愛

Trust God and Let God

Having experienced an intimate encounter with God's character, I was next asked to trust Him simply. Over the next season of my life, the following passage from Proverbs kept coming up.

> Trust in the Lord with all your heart, and lean not unto your understanding. In all your ways, acknowledge him, and he shall direct your paths.
>
> —Proverbs 3:5-6 NIV

God didn't want or need me to do anything to help Him along. He was quite capable of accomplishing His purposes, as His character revealed. I had to learn that God was grander than all my perceived impossible circumstances. Without infringing on the free will He'd given me, He was in control of all things, whether my small life or the entire universe. In short, I finally realized that I am not wiser than God!

Have you ever reached that conclusion? Looking back, I still can't believe I ever thought I knew more about how to handle my life than the God who created me. Maybe you don't consciously think as I did that you are wiser than God. But does your behavior show that is really how your mind thinks down deep? Speaking to His people through the prophet Isaiah, God stated very bluntly the comparison of His infinite wisdom to our paltry human wisdom.

> "My thoughts are nothing like your thoughts," says the LORD. "And my ways are far beyond anything you could imagine. For just as the heavens are higher than the earth, so my ways are higher than your ways and my thoughts higher than your thoughts."
>
> —Isaiah 55:8-9, NLT

So if God didn't want or need me to help Him along, what did He want with me? Slowly, I came to understand that God just wanted me to be in His loving presence. To enjoy spending time together as heavenly Father and daughter without being distracted by all the outside turmoil and trials of my life journey.

Have you ever had someone excited to be spending time with you but your own mind, body, and spirit did not engage with them? My daughters were the ones who really taught me the difference between occupying the same physical space and truly being in the presence of a loved one.

How can you tell if you are fully in someone's presence? Here are a few questions to ask in making that determination. Are you actually enjoying your time together? Do you laugh? Are you focused on that moment and the person you are with, or are you looking at your phone or running through a to-do list in your thoughts? Does your body language and eye contact make the other person feel they have your full attention?

Too often we can be in the same room with a spouse, family member, or friend we claim to love, sitting on a couch together, even engaged in conversation. But our minds and/or spirits are occupied with something other than really connecting with the person in whose physical presence we find ourselves.

Sadly, we are often that way with God also. We may be sitting in a church service or at home reading the Bible, but we are disengaged in mind and spirit. We are just going through the motions like checking another item off our to-do list.

To truly experience being in God's presence, I discovered that it helped to find a quiet place where I could be alone with

God. This may be sitting outside on a sunny day or enjoying a starry night with a bright moon amazed by the beauty of God's creation. Other times it means finding a quiet place indoors, dimming the lights, and meditating on God's words against a backdrop of peaceful gospel music. The more I take time to be in God's presence, the more I grow to intimately know God.

If fully experiencing and enjoying God's loving presence remains a challenge for you, consider taking the following simple steps that have helped me.

- Find a place and time where you can be alone with God.

- Intentionally quiet your mind, putting away any thoughts of the unfinished items on your to-do list.

- Take some deep breaths. With each breath, visualize your-self breathing out (releasing) your worries and breathing in (receiving) God's warm love.

- Visualize your loving heavenly Father embracing you and you hugging Him back.

- As you calm your mind, just be still and be there in God's presence.

- Repeat as often as needed, if possible at least once a day.

But it isn't enough just to sit in quiet solitude with God, no matter how wonderful the thoughts and images of God's love and presence. Enjoying fellowship with a loved one isn't just being in each other's presence. It also involves communication. And God showed me two other vital elements of developing a close intimate relationship with our heavenly Father.

The first is letting God speak directly to us through the power of His Word. We've talked about how God's ways and thoughts are as much higher than our ways and thoughts as the heavens (or all of outer space!) is higher than the earth (Isaiah 55:8-9). God goes on in that same passage to talk about the power of His Word.

> The rain and snow come down from the heavens and stay on the ground to water the earth. They cause the grain to grow, producing seed for the farmer and bread for the hungry. It is the same with my word. I send it out, and it always produces fruit. It will accomplish all I want it to, and it will prosper everywhere I send it. You will live in joy and peace. The mountains and hills will burst into song, and the trees of the field will clap their hands! Where once there were thrones, cypress trees will grow. Where nettles grew, myrtles will sprout up. These events will bring great honor to the LORDS's name; they will be an everlasting sign of his power and love.
>
> —Isaiah 55:10-13, NLT

What God is letting us know here is that God's Word working through His will for us will produce fruit in our lives if we will but follow God obediently through the Holy Spirit's guidance. It will also cause us to have lives abounding in joy and peace. We will see cypress trees growing in our lives where once there were thorns. And as we already saw in Romans 8:28, God's Word will accomplish all God wants to do, and that includes working all things "for the good of those who love Him."

The other important element of an intimate relationship with God is the power of prayer. God's Word is our heavenly Father speaking to His children. Prayer is His children speaking to their heavenly Father. And no topic is off-limits between a child and a loving parent, as we see in the below verses.

> Don't worry about anything; instead, pray about everything. Tell God what you need, and thank him for all he has done and will do.
>
> —Philippians 4:6, NLT

> If any of you lacks wisdom, you should ask God, who gives generously to all without finding fault, and it will be given to you.
>
> —James 1:5 NIV

As I began applying what God was showing me through His Word, I started bringing God my concerns and fears. I made a list of things I was thankful for and took time to give God thanks for each one, however small. I asked God for direction on issues where I needed clarity and guidance. I pleaded for His help and provision. And one by one, I began seeing God answer prayer and meet my requests, especially my need for help with my kids and finances.

God also brought new friends into my life that provided comfort and support. Let me just say a few words here about the importance and blessing of having friends who understand the heart of God and who lean on God. God created us to fellowship with others, and one of the wonderful blessings of spending time with other brothers and sisters in God's family is that our connection is at a spiritual level so that we just "get" each other.

The Bible has many examples of how we can spend quality time with others, show compassion, encourage each other in times of challenge, and build each other up through godly speech.

> And let us consider how we may spur one another on toward love and good deeds, not giving up meeting together, as some are in the habit of doing, but encouraging one another—and all the more as you see the Day approaching.
>
> —Hebrews 10:24-25 NIV

> But encourage one another daily, as long as it is called "Today," so that none of you may be hardened by sin's deceitfulness.
>
> —Hebrews 3:13 NIV

Do not let any unwholesome talk come out of your mouths, but only what is helpful for building others up according to their needs, that it may benefit those who listen.

—Ephesians 4:29 NIV

God also knows that believers aren't perfect. As we spend time together, we will inevitably have disagreements. But even this can be used positively for our spiritual growth so long as interpersonal conflict is handled biblically (Matthew 18:15-20). Part of being a loving community in positive relationship with each other is both welcoming and being willing to give constructive advice that is rooted in motives of genuine Christian love with each other's best interest at heart. As we keep ourselves in God's Word, we can help keep each other on God's path, as King Solomon so wisely stated.

As iron sharpens iron, so one person sharpens another.

—Proverbs 27:17 NIV

Going back to that next step God put in front of me at the beginning of this chapter that I should trust Him simply, I had long known in my head that those who trust God and follow the leading of the Holy Spirit will therefore be alive in God. But my life hadn't reflected that until I came to truly know the character of my heavenly Father and live increasingly in the intimacy of His presence.

One way in which I learned to sense and follow the Holy Spirit's leading was actually through my ballroom dancing. In ballroom dancing, I had to learn to sense my partner's prompting through the tiniest movements of his arms, hands, feet, and body and follow his lead. When I began ballroom dancing, I didn't sense my partner's prompting and would often try to lead instead of following.

But as I became increasingly aware of his prompting and yielded to his lead, my partner and I were able to flow smoothly and beautifully across the dance floor as one unit. God taught me to apply this lesson in becoming more aware of the Holy Spirit's nudging, leading, and prompting. As I began obeying that prompting and leading, I grew in intimacy and oneness with God in both heart and actions.

Maybe you've experienced similar struggles along your life journey. Maybe you are experiencing them now. Are you barely surviving one day at a time, or are you thriving in God's love, peace, and grace that overflow from your heart into other people's lives. Are you trying to fend for yourself in your own way according to what makes sense to you, or are you asking God to show you through the Holy Spirit what He has planned for you the next moment in time? Do your moment by moment circumstances changes your mood, or are you excited and at peace with what the Holy Spirit is prompting you?

I pray with you now that your answer on each of these questions will be the latter and that God's Holy Spirit will make you alive in God as you follow His leading.

FIFTEEN

信望愛

MORE GOD LESSONS

As I grew in intimacy with God and learned to be still in His presence, God's Holy Spirit was working in my life in other ways, teaching me spiritual lessons that were vital to the process of transforming from that caterpillar stuck crawling along the ground to an exquisite butterfly taking flight with its new wings. The list is unending, but let me share a few that were especially necessary before I could move forward in my spiritual journey and daily life.

Forgiving Myself

Imagine you've forgiven a friend for a wrong they've done to you, but that friend still repeatedly comes to you and asks for your forgiveness. Does that even make sense? That is precisely what I was doing when I was unable to accept that Jesus had already forgiven me. For many years, I felt I had to continue carrying my mistakes as heavy burdens. I didn't connect that God had already forgiven me of all my mistakes through Jesus's death on the cross when He took on Himself the full penalty for my sins so I didn't need to keep carrying these burdens any longer.

Have you learned to forgive others but haven't forgiven yourself? Do you find yourself continuing to wrap the burden of guilt and shame around yourself like a security blanket? If so, please know that Jesus has already taken up your load. Do you really think your mistakes could possibly be bigger and greater than God's capacity to forgive? Or maybe you believe God's forgiveness is not good enough for you. Believe me, it isn't humility but pride and arrogance to ever think your mistake is greater than God can forgive!

These are some of the struggles and questions I had to work through myself. I came to the realization that God is not just sitting on His throne in heaven looking for opportunities to give me a hard time or condemn me for having messed up once again. God sent His only Son to die for me. That is amazing love! My misperception needed to realign itself with God's truth, which is that God has already forgiven me so now it was my turn to forgive myself.

The following verses instruct us to forgive as we ourselves have been forgiven and permanently freed through Christ from condemnation. That forgiveness isn't meant to be extended just to other people but also to ourselves.

> Instead, be kind to each other, tenderhearted, forgiving one another, just as God through Christ has forgiven you.
>
> —Ephesians 4:32 NIV

> And, now there is no condemnation for those who belong to Christ Jesus.
>
> —Romans 8:1, NLT

Valuing Myself

If you've ever been on a plane, you will remember the attendant advising, "In case of an emergency, put your own oxygen mask on first before you help put a mask on others." This may sound selfish. But the instruction actually highlights an important principle that if you don't first meet your own needs, in this case for oxygen, you quite literally won't have the breath to help meet the needs of others.

What does it mean to value yourself? Maybe you've spent much of your lifetime caring for and loving others but have always felt it was selfish to spend even a few minutes caring for and loving yourself. I'm not talking about self-indulgence. There is a balance. But to truly love others unconditionally, we need to first value ourselves as God does. We need to believe in our hearts that God loves us unconditionally. How can you really love others if you've never received God's unconditional love?

I'm not talking about receiving Jesus into your heart just to be saved but receiving God's love to begin a wonderful and beautiful relationship with Him.

Jesus Himself taught this principle when a legal expert asked Him what was the most important commandment given in Scripture.

> Jesus replied: "'Love the Lord your God with all your heart and with all your soul and with all your mind.' This is the first and greatest commandment. And the second is like it: 'Love your neighbor as yourself.' All the Law and the Prophets hang on these two commandments."
>
> —Matthew 22:37-40 NIV
>
> see also Mark 12:28-31

Notice the order laid out in this passage of Scripture. We are first to love God above all else. Second is a presumption that we love ourselves. Third, we are to love others *as* we love ourselves. We aren't told to love others *more* than we love ourselves.

These verses and this progression indicate how God wants us to value ourselves in order to receive His love. If the value you place on yourself is so low that you don't believe you are worthy of God loving you, how then can you receive His love? But as you learn to love yourself because you see yourself as the valuable, precious child God created, then you will be increasingly able to receive God's beautiful, warm love that has been waiting for you.

And as God's love fills us up to overflowing, we can then love our neighbors as we've learned to love and value ourselves.

Consider closing your eyes right now and asking yourself, "Do I sense God's love embrace in the deepest part of my heart?" Answer honestly right where you are. Then reach out to God and visualize His open arms giving you a big embrace and His loving voice saying, "My dear, I already loved you even before you were born. You are precious and dear to Me. I have been and will always be alongside you."

Forgiving Others

Now that I was learning to forgive and value myself, God showed me that He wanted me to forgive others. He brought to my attention a verse that at first confused me.

> But when you are praying, first forgive anyone you are holding a grudge against, so that your Father in heaven will forgive your sins, too.
>
> —Mark 11:25, NLT
>
> see also Matthew 6:14-15

"What does that even mean, God?" I asked. Was this passage saying that God would revoke His forgiveness of my sins and my salvation in Jesus Christ if I developed a grudge against someone? Not at all, if the verse is read in context of other biblical teaching. The context here of prayer does mean that unkindness, unforgiveness, and other disobedience to God's commands can close down our communication with God and hinder His response to our prayers (Psalm 66:18; Isaiah 59:2; John 9:31; James 4:2; 1 Peter 3:7).

Through time, I came to realize that refusing to address the pain I'd buried deep down inside or the need to forgive those who'd caused that pain had molded me into someone who was not God's intended plan for me. Constantly holding onto hurt, pain, anger, and sadness became ingrained in my thoughts and even in very cells in my body. It began defining who I was.

Looking back to when I became a mother, I also saw how these emotions had affected my daughters. A year after the divorce, I recognized that I'd continued to be bitter and angry, was still keeping a list of offenses, and had health issues due to not dealing with my emotions. I wasn't able to let go of the deep pain and trauma of the divorce. This wasn't just an obstacle in healing my heart but was affecting my girls. During my second year attending the divorce care sessions, God started opening my heart and healing the hurt, pain, betrayals, and resentments. God also began teaching me to accept people where they are by showing me that we are all sinners.

Then I experienced another wonderful God intervention. Though I'd lived in this neighborhood for over ten years, I'd never visited a particular nearby hair salon. One day I did stop in. While there, I met a very kind, motherly woman who was also divorced with kids. As we talked, she shared how her husband had left her, had a child with another woman, then through a marriage reconciliation program the couple had been reconciled. This woman's heart was so warm and loving that she'd not only welcomed her husband back into her life but embraced his new child as well.

Recognizing my continued hurt and bitterness, this kindly woman invited me to attend the marriage reconciliation class with her, which met at an area church. She further explained that the class didn't focus primarily on reconciling with an ex-spouse but on reconciling first with God. If this led to a marriage getting reconciled, great. But even if that didn't occur, reconciling and building a closer relationship with God was the most important priority.

I no longer had any hope of marriage reconciliation, so my first reaction was to dismiss her invitation. But over the following weeks, God kept bringing it back to my mind. Finally about three months later, I visited the class. As with the divorce care class, each person shared their invitation. Some were still married but going through a lot of marriage problems. Others were separated or already divorced.

I ended up attending this class for the next three-plus years, and it became another important step in my spiritual growth. During this time, I did work out a lot of anger and resentment.

As God continued working on my heart, I was finally able to fully grasp God's grace and love for us, despite how imperfect we are. God doesn't seek for us to be perfect but to be willing. God desires us to forgive others.

When I was finally able to let go of deeply held negative emotions, I was also able to forgive. That forgiveness allowed me to surrender my negative feelings and hurts to God, which in turn began healing my heart and soul so that I could move forward toward the future of who God plans for me to be. The Holy Spirit revealed that forgiveness doesn't mean forgetting, nor does it mean condoning or excusing offenses. But forgiveness brought me peace of mind and freed me from the corrosive anger and sadness that had blocked my path to my purpose.

Have you ever felt you've been carrying large boulders of past pain, hurt, and resentments that weigh your life down to a point where there is nothing joyful in your life? Have you become so bitter and angry it is hard for people to be around you? Maybe you are saying right now as you read this, "Don't you even realize what they did to me?"

Yes, I do! But harboring unforgiveness is how you imprison yourself. Taking your life back so that you can thrive instead of barely surviving requires that you take the step of forgiving those who hurt you in the past. I love these words of renowned

Christian author Lewis B. Smedes from his book *Forgive and Forget: Healing the Hurts We Don't Deserve*.

> To forgive is to set a prisoner free and discover that the prisoner was you.

Right now take a moment and visualize the person who hurt you locked up in a prison where you've placed them because they haven't apologized for their wrong against you. Of course this means that you as the prison guard must stay there to keep watch over the prisoner. Similarly, your unforgiving thoughts and negative emotions are keeping you chained to past pains and hurt to the point that it impacts your physical body and can even cause serious illness. This state of mind doesn't hurt the other person at all, so you end up just hurting and imprisoning yourself.

That said, forgiving someone doesn't mean we should be expected to blindly trust them again. In fact, the Gospels tell us that Jesus Himself did not blindly trust people because He knew exactly what was in their hearts and minds.

> But Jesus didn't trust them because he knew all about people.
> —John 2:24, NLT

Instead, we are encouraged to place our trust in God, who will never fail us or break His Word as Scripture repeatedly reminds us.

> It is better to take refuge in the LORD than to trust in princes.
> —Psalm 118:9 NIV

Trust in the LORD with all your heart and lean not on your own understanding; in all your ways submit to him, and he will make your paths straight.

—Proverbs 3:5-6 NIV

God's way is perfect. All the LORD's promises prove true. He is a shield for all who look to him for protection.

—Psalm 18:30, NLT

Not Judging

As I learned to forgive, God was also teaching me another lesson—to leave judging others or my concerns about seeing justice done to my all-wise and just heavenly Father.

Do not judge, and you will not be judged. Do not condemn, and you will not be condemned. Forgive, and you will be forgiven.

—Luke 6:37 NIV

For the Lord is our judge, the Lord is our lawgiver, the Lord is our king; it is he who will save us.

—Isaiah 33:2 NIV

And will not God bring about justice for his chosen ones, who cry out to him day and night?

—Luke 18:7 NIV

see also Ecclesiastes 3:17; Isaiah 61:8; Romans 2:16

God reassured me that since He is the judge of each person's life and will deal with all injustice, we can leave the injustices we've experienced at the altar. We no longer have to carry the offense. Although it is normal for us to feel anger toward sin and injustice, it is not our job to judge others, carry out justice, or ensure fairness. In fact, God may choose a very different plan for the offending person's life than what we might have in mind. In God's eyes, the best outcome is for that person to repent and come to Christ. In so doing, God may use their story to help others know Jesus.

But even as I processed these God-lessons, I battled fear over how to move forward in the next phase of my life, whether in relationships, motherhood, career, or other areas of life. What if I got hurt again? What if my interests weren't being protected?

Once again, I was letting my anxiety and fear take over. As had been the pattern of my life, I wanted to remain in control. Of course that was an illusion. We are never really in control. I had to let God be God, trusting that God would take care of these matters and that God's care was sufficient for the situation. I had to arrive at a state where I asked God these words.

> Search me, God, and know my heart; test me and know my anxious thoughts. See if there is any offensive way in me, and lead me in the way everlasting.
>
> —Psalm 139:23-24 NIV

Sixteen

信望愛

Waiting for God

G od was also working on my need for patience. I've mentioned the verse God gave me about learning to be still and know that He is God (Psalm 46:10) when I was first learning His true character and how to abide in His presence. But sitting still and just patiently waiting for God to act instead of getting out there and trying to take control myself isn't something that comes naturally to me. The Holy Spirit brought to my attention how many times in the Bible we are told to wait patiently for God's timing and plan of action.

> Wait patiently for the LORD. Be brave and courageous. Yes, wait patiently for the LORD.
>
> —Psalms 27:14, NLT

> Be still in the presence of the LORD and wait patiently for him to act.
>
> —Psalm 37:7a, NLT

The Lord will fight for you; you need only to be still.

—Exodus 14:14 NIV

Yet the Lord longs to be gracious to you; therefore he will rise up to show you compassion. For the Lord is a God of justice. Blessed are all who wait for him!

—Isaiah 30:18 NIV

Many times and in different circumstances, God asked me to wait patiently for His timing. One day, He showed me a beautiful double rainbow as a reminder that His promise is coming just as He'd placed the first rainbow in the clouds as a reminder of God's everlasting covenant with Noah and all of us who have descended from Noah (Genesis 9:12-16). Though there were still clouds in the sky, my storm was passing, and God was restoring my brokenness (Psalm 147:3) and all years that the locusts had stolen from me (Joel 2:25).

So what do you do while you are waiting on God? Well, what do you do when you are waiting for another human being? While you wait, are you occupying yourself with other activities? Waiting for God is not a *passive* act but an *active* one. While you are waiting, God is seeking to reconnect with you. This isn't easy, especially if you are used to being on the go all the time. But this is a time when God wants to build a one-on-one loving relationship with you. It isn't about Bible knowledge but spending time to understand our heavenly Father's heart for you and His deep unconditional love.

As you wait on God, your senses will be opened to recognize how God is speaking to you and wanting to connect with you. Are there different ways through which He is bringing you His love messages? I mentioned before how God spoke love to me through a church billboard as well as through movies, music, other people, books, and other material I've read.

During this time of waiting on God, you will also be challenged on what you believe about yourself and others. Satan will bring doubt and come at you with spiritual warfare. Arm yourself with God's Word and surround yourself with a group of prayer warriors. Build your dependency on God and the Holy Spirit's leading.

God will also use this time of waiting to transform you. This may be a difficult process like the caterpillar struggling to shed its old body and cocoon. But when you look back on it, you'll realize this was among the sweetest times of your life. God may not show you too far ahead down the road because He desires you to trust in who He is. Too much of the big picture can also become overwhelming and daunting, paralyzing us from ever taking the first step. I've found that I am only able to continue in God's freedom with the help of Holy Spirit.

> For the Lord is the Spirit, and wherever the Spirit of the Lord is, there is freedom. So all of us who have had that veil removed can see and reflect the glory of the Lord. And the Lord—who is

the Spirit—makes us more and more like him as we are changed into his glorious image.

—2 Corinthians 3:17-18, NLT

While transformation is a sometimes painful journey with many struggles, it is also an amazing one if you are willing to step forward and embrace what God has planned for the next stage of your life. When we can't see things changing with our naked eye, that doesn't mean nothing is happening. Our time of waiting on God is like the winter season when on the surface nothing is happening but under the surface nature is preparing for the new birth of spring activities.

In the same way, changes may be happening in your heart or spirit, your mental thoughts, your internal body, etc., that are not easily detected by the naked eye. Your healing is preparing your mind, body, and spirit to spring forth when you enter your next amazing stage of life. God is very interested in our transformation as His Word speaks of it often and calls for us to pursue that transformation.

Do not conform to the pattern of this world, but be transformed by the renewing of your mind. Then you will be able to test and approve what God's will is—his good, pleasing and perfect will.

—Romans 12:2 NIV

Throw off your old sinful nature and your former way of life, which is corrupted by lust and deception. Instead, let the Spirit renew your thoughts and attitudes. Put on your new nature, created to be like God—truly righteous and holy.

—Ephesians 4:22-24, NLT

How do we pursue transformation? We must intentionally throw off our past way of life and sinful nature and intentionally allow our mind and thoughts to be renewed by the Holy Spirit. How aware are you of your thought life or your relationship with God? As you allow the Holy Spirit to work, you are able to tap into many resources to continue your healing and strengthen your mind, thoughts, spirit, and heart.

These are amazing steps many people never arrive at because it takes an intentional investment of time and commitment. But it is a worthwhile investment that will not only benefit you in many ways but allow you to help others by sharing with them how God has helped you, as I discovered sharing my own story in that divorce care class.

Are you perhaps at this very moment on the edge of your breakthrough? Your patience with yourself and willingness to transform will be a great blessing to you and others. Your transformation from a caterpillar to an amazing, gorgeous butterfly is like shedding an old coat from the past and preparing for the growth of a beautiful new you.

Seventeen

信望愛

Embracing
God's Healing

One day while I was still attending the marriage reconciliation classes, a woman shared her story of how God had worked in her life and she'd ended up reconciling with her ex-husband after nine years of separation. They were remarried ten years after their original divorce. Each time she shared her story in following classes, the timeframe of her story jumped out at me. I began asking God what He was trying to say to me.

"You need to wait for ten years before pursuing another relationship," God's Holy Spirit spoke clearly to my heart.

"Are you sure?" I responded, still not having completely learned to stop arguing with my Creator. "That is a long wait!"

During my divorce care classes, I'd seen many people who were recently divorced jump right into another relationship instead of working on their issues and relationship with God. The new relationship inevitably encountered great challenges and usually failed. But ten years? I didn't think I needed that much time to heal. But apparently God did!

It has now been just about exactly ten years since the divorce. During those years, I've come to fully embrace how much God has loved me over my entire life even when I wasn't seeing it and how much He continues to love me. I've learned to lean on God daily for what He has planned for me. I've come to distinguish the whisper of the Holy Spirit.

I've also come to recognize that as we walk closer to God and His will, we will encounter an increase in life challenges because these are rooted in spiritual battles. This is why it is so important that we put on God's spiritual armor, as the apostle Paul describes in depth in his epistle to the Ephesian church. If we are to take our stand against the devil and fight effectively against spiritual forces of evil, we must first put on the protection of God's armor, then wield the weapons of our spiritual warfare—the sword of God's Word and constant prayer in the Spirit.

Put on the full armor of God, so that you can take your stand against the devil's schemes. For our struggle is not against flesh and blood, but against the rulers, against the authorities, against the powers of this dark world and against the spiritual forces of evil in the heavenly realms . . . Stand firm then, with the belt of truth buckled around your waist, with the breastplate of righteousness in place, and with your feet fitted with the readiness that comes from the gospel of peace. In addition to all this, take up the shield of faith, with which you can extinguish all the flaming arrows of the evil one. Take the helmet of salvation and the sword of the Spirit, which is the word of God. And pray in the Spirit on all occasions with all kinds of prayers and requests.

—Ephesians 6:11-18b NIV

During this same time period, God showed me that the connection between our spiritual, emotional, and mental self and our physical bodies is very much interconnected and complex. He not only forgives our sins but created our body to heal itself, which I am very grateful. The Old Testament book of Isaiah gives us King Hezekiah's prayer after God healed him miraculously through the word of the prophet Isaiah (see also 2 Kings 20).

You restored me to health and let me live. Surely it was for my benefit that I suffered such anguish. In your love, you kept me from the pit of destruction; you have put all my sins behind your back."

—Isaiah 38:16b-17 NIV

God showed me how our illnesses can originate from negative suppressed emotions. As the Holy Spirit brought to my mind certain suppressed emotions and past experiences that had caused my emotional pain, I was able to release many of these negative suppressed emotions through holistic healing techniques God led me to learn while trying to help a friend who was also dealing with negative emotional baggage that was affecting his health. It is amazing how God opened my eyes to how the knowledge my parents had learned in studying eastern massage techniques, including our body's acupressure points and organ meridians, are integrated in this healing technique.

God has shown me that holistic healing involves all levels—spiritual, emotional, mental, and social as well as physical. Over time, God slowly healed various aspects of my own emotional pain and past negative experiences. As my spiritual, emotional, and mental illnesses were healed, that spilled over into healing my body and improving my overall physical health.

One major area where God healed was my anger, pain, and resentment toward my ex-husband and parents so that I could finally accept and love them where they are and for who they are. I had prayed for reconciliation with my dad as God had given me with my mom. In 2015, Dad called and asked for me to come to Taiwan to attend the fortieth anniversary celebration of his non-profit educational society for the blind. I traveled there with my oldest daughter, who was eleven, and my second daughter, who was turning five, as well as a close friend from the divorce care class. Dad had met my oldest daughter before, but this was his first time to meet my second daughter.

It meant a lot to Dad that I'd traveled so far to support him in this way. He proudly introduced me to the mayor and councilmembers of Taipei. He asked me to give some words of thanks in English at the anniversary celebration, and my friend who'd come with me spoke as well. During our visit, Dad also bonded in a special way with my second daughter. He was very playful, and they really enjoyed each other.

I was happy Dad was able to bond with my little one, but I was also struggling with deep resentment that he'd been absent all the years when I'd needed his support and had shown no real desire to connection with my brothers and me as he'd bonded with my second daughter. Then it occurred to me that this was very similar to my relationship with my own dear A-gong, who hadn't bonded with his own son but had done so with me as his granddaughter.

Later in 2018, Mom broke her arm while getting the non-profit ready for a Christmas celebration. Caring for her and the non-profit became too much for my dad, so he called me to see if I could fly out there to help him with my mom. I did so. While I was there, Dad and I had a serious discussion about faith for the first time in my life. He asked me why God allowed suffering. I was shocked since he was the one who had attended seminary.

I responded by reminding him that God has given us free will. Some bad things happen due to our own decisions, and some happen due to other people's decisions. But God is always there with us through our trials if we are willing to acknowledge Him. God never abandons us. I shared with him several examples from my own Himalayan mountain peak experiences, including the car accident, muggings, and surgeries.

That said, sometimes we are surrounded by love but focus so much on ourselves that we are unable to feel that love. It is hard to convince someone they are loved when they keep pushing away the love. I went on to share with my experience with my first college boyfriend and how I hadn't felt worthy of being loved by someone like him so I'd kept pushing him away. Similarly, my perception of whether I was worthy to be loved affected my perspective of understanding who I was as a child of God. Was I the precious adopted daughter of the King through Jesus? Or did I still see myself as a worthless sinner beyond redemption even though I'd accepted Jesus into my heart?

Dad understood what I was trying to say, and after this talk, I felt God had shown him that I loved him unconditionally right where he is at just as God loves me unconditionally. From that point on, God greatly reconciled our relationship, and we began bonding in a way we never had before. The first time Dad said "I love you" out loud was like that first hug I'd given him before me heading off to college. It is still hard for him to verbalize the words as he wasn't raised that way. But every time I speak to him, I tell him, "Dad, I love you."

Dad calls more often since the Covid-19 pandemic started, always wanting to make sure everyone is healthy and that we have enough masks and other supplies. While both of my parents are still managing the non-profit in Taiwan, they are planning to move back together to the United States within the next year or so to be closer to all their children and grandchildren. My old brother Jeff now has three children, and my younger brother George has four along with my two, so our family here in the United States is growing.

Meanwhile, my relationship with my ex-husband has remained cordial. We've shared custody with the girls, and the amount of time he spends with them has increased as they grow older, which has permitted them to build a strong relationship with their father. He has always been very involved in the girls' lives and been a very loving dad to the girls. My oldest daughter is heading off to college. My younger daughter is heading to middle-school, and she loves horses. I pray for both of them that God will guide them to His plan for their future.

Meanwhile, I continue working at the Fort Worth Water Department and being a single mom. My walk with God and leaning on Holy Spirit have continued to grow stronger. In obedience to God's word on my heart, I haven't dated since my divorce. But several years ago, I reconnected with an old friend from the University of Texas. He'd graduated from the architecture engineering program and had ended up with an engineering firm in Fort Worth. I'd invited him to the young professionals group at the church I was attending, and we'd been good friends for several years before I'd begun dating my husband. About that time, he'd moved to another state to study photography, and we'd lost touch.

In 2017, we reconnected on social media. For all I knew he could have been married with several kids and a happy life. And I reminded myself that the ten years weren't up. However, I kept feeling the urge of the Holy Spirit to reach out. When we did reconnect, I discovered he too had been through a lot of trials and trauma, including divorce, loss of his father, and a serious health crisis. I was able to share with him the God-lessons I'd been through as well as some of the holistic healing techniques that were so helpful in my own emotional, physical, and spiritual healing.

He has since moved back to the Fort Worth area. Over the last few years, our friendship has developed as God has continued to heal both of us from past pain and trauma. And as God has taught me how to love others compassionately, I have also witnessed my friend's heart and spirit opening up to God's love for him. I respect God's decision and timing, and I know that whatever happens in our future is in our best interest because God's plan is always perfect and the most beneficial for our lives.

Meanwhile, I have every confidence and peace that God has a great plan ahead for me, and I cannot wait to walk with God for the next chapters of my life, whatever those may be.

EIGHTEEN

信望愛

FORWARD-MOVING FAITH

So where do we go from here? Some of you may be hesitating in moving forward toward God's plan for your life out of fear of taking the wrong next step. I can definitely relate as I go through this struggle a lot. From early childhood, I chose to learn from others' mistakes so that I didn't have to learn hard lessons through making mistakes of my own. I would prepare as much as possible to avoid mistakes and inefficiencies.

Do you fear making mistakes to the point that you are left standing frozen in your path? I've done that many times also. But this is why God sent the Holy Spirit to guide us. As we pray to God and seek His next step, we may face uncertainty and wonder if we are hearing God correctly. But what God desires from us is that we be willing, and He will work out the rest.

We see this demonstrated in Acts 16 when the apostle Paul and his companions made plans to travel to certain parts of Asia to preach the gospel. But as they came to the various regions of Phrygia, Galatia, Mysia, and Bithynia, the Holy Spirit repeatedly prevented them from preaching God's Word there (Acts 16:6-8).

In each of these places, Paul was taking a step toward what he thought was God's plan. When God had other plans, the Holy Spirit made this clear to Paul. Because Paul humbled himself in listening to the Holy Spirit and allowing himself to be redirected, God gave him a vision revealing that God's next step for Paul was to travel to Macedonia to preach the gospel there (Acts 16:9-10). The result of Paul's obedience was that the gospel spread into Europe as well as Asia.

I've already shared the following verses with you that God laid so strongly on my heart during the beginning of my season of waiting and being still, but let's read it one more time in a different version.

> Trust in the LORD with all your heart; do not depend on your own understanding. Seek His will in all you do, and He will show you which path to take.
>
> —Proverbs 3:5-6, NLT

When the timing of God's plan is different than our own plan, there may be a reason behind the scenes of which we aren't aware but God is. Sometimes God is working up ahead of us to prepare a path that isn't yet ready for us to travel. But whether or not we understand why the Holy Spirit is nudging us onto a different path, we can have absolute faith that God is there with us, as we also read earlier.

> Do not be afraid or discouraged, for the Lord will personally go ahead of you. He will be with you; He will neither fail you nor abandon you.
>
> —Deuteronomy 31:8, NLT

True faith always looks forward. When you place your trust in God, your security is in God's hands. Since God is eternal, your future is secure. Your assurance in stepping forward into the future or the unknown is based on trusting who God is and who He says He is. God sends the Holy Spirit to guide us toward the grander plan He has for us because He has our best interests in mind as the prophet Isaiah reminds.

> To bestow on them a crown of beauty instead of ashes, the oil of joy instead of mourning, and a garment of praise instead of a spirit of despair.
>
> —Isaiah 61:3 NIV

We are each God's masterpiece. Our life may feel like broken pieces, but God has assembled those broken pieces into beautiful stained-glass art to demonstrate how He will use even our brokenness to heal us. There is gratitude in realizing how the stained-glass art of our life gives us confidence that God will continue to be there to heal, guide, provide, and carry us through life's challenges. Our stained-glass mosaic of broken pieces also gives hope to others who are going through similar challenges.

That said, we need to keep in mind that stepping forward into faith is not easy and may require baby steps at times. God gave us free will, and at many varying places along our life journey, God reaches out and provides us opportunities to follow His path. The question is what we will do with that free will. Do we weigh how much benefit we would get from obediently taking those steps of following God? Or do we weigh only what we perceive as benefiting us? The apostle Paul gave stern admonishment as to how we should be using the freedom we have in Christ.

> For you have been called to live in freedom, my brothers and sisters. But don't use your freedom to satisfy your sinful nature. Instead, use your freedom to serve one another in love.
>
> —Galatians 5:13, NLT

Below are several examples from Scripture where various individuals were given the opportunity to make an impact for the greater good of God's kingdom.

- *Ruth 1:16*: Ruth had to decide whether to stay in her birth nation of Moab, an idolatrous culture, or go with her mother-in-law Naomi to Bethlehem in Israel, in so doing choosing to also follow Naomi's God. Ruth decided to follow Naomi, and because of her choice she became part of the genealogy of Jesus.

- *John 12:27-28*: Jesus had to decide whether or not to willingly sacrifice Himself for our sins. Jesus chose to die on the cross for us and fulfill God's plan of being our Savior.

- *Matthew 1:20*: Joseph had to decide whether to follow the angel's instructions in taking Mary, who was pregnant by the Holy Spirit, as his wife. Joseph chose to take Mary as his wife and became Jesus's legal father.

- *Mark 10:17-21*: The rich man had to decide whether or not to give up his possessions and follow Jesus. He decided his riches were too great to give up, thereby forgoing amazing opportunities and a life journey with Jesus.

In these examples, the first three decided to follow God, but the last one did not as the amount of sacrifice involved seemed too great. I shared in a previous chapter of God's invitation to me after I graduated from the University of Texas when God made so abundantly clear I was to follow Him back to Dallas. At the time, I had to decide to follow God or pursue my own desires to stay in Austin near my friends and away from my family.

I chose to follow God's invitation, and despite many challenges, it has been an amazing journey. God blessed me with a marriage situation that resulted in reconciling me to God and learning to lean on God. It gave me my two loving sweetheart daughters, many friendships, and an amazing twenty-plus-year career with the City of Fort Worth Water Department. And I have absolute faith there is much more is to come.

God also told me many times to just share what He has done in my life and tell my story so that others will be encouraged. God has a way of using the Holy Spirit to nudge me to share at certain moments.

> So I say, let the Holy Spirit guide your lives. Then you won't be doing what your sinful nature craves.
>
> —Galatians 5:16, NLT

I've noticed that when I resist the Holy Spirit's prompting, He tends to ramp up the "gentle urging." Many times in the past, my fear of speaking and worry over how others perceive me have caused me to miss an opportunity of sharing and of allowing God to use me at that moment. God has said to me, "Do not make this bigger than what I asked for you to do." Then as I obediently tell my story to the best of my own ability, God will bless someone by using what I've shared to help facilitate their healing.

God invites us to walk through His open door and step forward onto the path of His plan for our lives. This will not be easy and may not even make sense by any worldly measure. will cause you to grow and mature. God will be there with you. He will give you strength when you are weak. His blessings for you at the other end of the door are going to be amazing.

So how do we know if we are experiencing God's freedom? God brought the following passage to my attention.

> But the Holy Spirit produces this kind of fruit in our lives: love, joy, peace, patience, kindness, goodness, faithfulness, gentleness, and self-control. There is no law against such things!
>
> —Galatians 5:22-23, NLT

Notice it says there is no law against love, joy, peace, and all the other wonderful fruits the Holy Spirit produces in our lives. So if your life is demonstrating those fruits, then you can be assured you are experiencing God's freedom. Likewise, if we are wondering whether we are really experiencing and demonstrating God's love, we need only read the following passage. If we are demonstrating these characteristics in our lives, then we are displaying God's love.

> Love is patient, love is kind. It does not envy, it does not boast, it is not proud. It does not dishonor others, it is not self-seeking, it is not easily angered, it keeps no record of wrongs. Love does not delight in evil but rejoices with the truth. It always protects, always trusts, always hopes, and always perseveres.
>
> —1 Corinthians 13:4-7 NIV

I am so blessed to have a restored relationship with my heavenly Father. I still have much growth ahead of me. But I am continuously getting to know Him better, and I've come to understand better God's perspective in working ahead of what we can see from our human perspective. He loves us all as His children and wants us to be free in Him. Having spiritual freedom means having peace and acknowledging that God owns everything and is in control of everything. We are simply stewards of what He provides to us.

God revealed to me that even during my time of rebellion, He still provided for me. He still loved me. But God has also allowed me to experience the consequences of my choices when I've chosen to do other things than what the Holy Spirit has gently directed me to do. This is God's healthy boundary. He gave me my free will. God can and does work miracles. But He is waiting for my faith to catch up to believe He is capable. He is waiting for me to understand how truly big He is. If I am to receive the miracle God has already orchestrated for me, God requires me to take that first step of faith.

What is your next faith step in conquering the obstacle that has been blocking you from receiving the miracle God has planned for you? We are God's beautiful creation with great potential. We are also like God's book in which new chapters are constantly being created as we choose to partner with Him instead of leading our own lives. This partnership is not based on my own strength, knowledge, or effort. It is based on God as my foundation, Jesus as my Savior, and the Holy Spirit as my guide.

My maternal grandmother nurtured my mom back to health during her meningitis and many years of support afterward. My paternal grandparents helped my dad with his non-profit for the blind and with raising my brothers and me. The fruit of their nurturing and support provided my brothers and me with a good foundation so that we in turn could nurture our kids, the first generation of our family born in the United States.

But that doesn't begin to compare with God's love and nurturing support, which is beyond anything we could imagine. He is a loving Father, and He is waiting for you to make the next step. Your decision to journey with God and nurture this amazing relationship, beginning with accepting Jesus Christ as your Savior, is the first step toward many future generational blessings.

This brings me to the end of my story, the book God called me to write. With the help of the Holy Spirit, I have been obedient to that call, and I am so glad you took the time to allow me to share with you my journey through anger, bitterness, and brokenness to God's wonderful love, healing, and redemption. No matter which Himalayan mountain peak your own life trials may have you climbing right now, maybe even your own Mt. Everest that is higher and more difficult than any you've climbed before, I pray that you too will allow God's redemptive love to bring you His wonderful, abundant holistic healing—spiritually, emotionally, mentally, and physically.

Now it is your turn. The next chapters of *your* book are to be determined by *you* as *you* decide your next step. Freedom is your choice! Are you ready to lay claim to God's freedom in your life? It is my prayer that your answer will be a resounding yes! Let me leave you with one final scripture, benediction, and challenge from my heart to yours.

> May the Lord lead your heart into a full understanding and expression of the love of God and the patient endurance that comes from Christ
>
> —2 Thessalonians 3:5, NLT

If you are willing to share your story of how God is impacting your life or how you are reconciling with Him or if you need prayer, I would love to hear from you. Feel free to reach out to me at any time at www.WendyChi.com.

ABOUT THE AUTHOR

Author and speaker Wendy (Wen Hui) Chi graduated from the University of Texas in Austin with a bachelor's of science in civil engineering and an executive master's in business administration from University of Texas at Arlington. She is a licensed professional engineer, and continues to work in this field as an assistant director of strategic operations, in the state of Texas. She has two beautiful daughters and loves to encourage others through their journey of healing. She can be contacted at www.WendyChi.com.

Made in the USA
Columbia, SC
05 April 2022

58542972R00104